The Animal Rights Debate

ISSUES

Volume 3

Editor

Craig Donnellan

Independence

Educational Publishers
Cambridge

First published by Independence
PO Box 295
Cambridge CB1 3XP
England

© Craig Donnellan 2002

British Library Cataloguing in Publication Data
The Animal Rights Debate – (Issues Series)
I. Donnellan, Craig II. Series
179.3

ISBN 1 86168 201 8

Printed in Great Britain
The Burlington Press
Cambridge

Typeset by
Claire Boyd

Cover
The illustration on the front cover is by
Pumpkin House.

CONTENTS

Introduction

The Animal Rights Debate is the third volume in the Issues series. The aim of this series is to offer up-to-date information about important issues in our world.

The Animal Rights Debate examines animal welfare and cruelty, animals used in experiments and the debate on fox-hunting.

The information comes from a wide variety of sources and includes:
Government reports and statistics
Newspaper reports and features
Magazine articles and surveys
Literature from lobby groups
and charitable organisations.

It is hoped that, as you read about the many aspects of the issues explored in this book, you will critically evaluate the information presented. It is important that you decide whether you are being presented with facts or opinions. Does the writer give a biased or an unbiased report? If an opinion is being expressed, do you agree with the writer?

The Animal Rights Debate offers a useful starting-point for those who need convenient access to information about the many issues involved. However, it is only a starting-point. At the back of the book is a list of organisations which you may want to contact for further information.

*****

Animal welfare

A non-religious perspective on animal welfare. Information from the British Humanist Association (BHA)

Most reasonable people think that we ought to treat other people well, that we should respect their rights and consider their welfare. But should we also treat other animals well, and why should we? Do they, too, have rights that we should respect? Humanists (non-religious people guided by moral principles based on reason and respect for others, not obedience to dogmatic rules) have no 'party line' on animal welfare, and no compulsory customs or religious food taboos that would influence their attitude to animals. They have to think for themselves, and decide whether to extend their concern for welfare from humans to animals. Humanists tend to put the needs of human beings first if there is a conflict, and to value animals and the natural world for human-centred reasons. But a rational non-religious morality, based on observation and experience, is likely to include an unwillingness to cause animals suffering, based on respect and affection for them.

Different cultures, different views

The debate about how we treat animals has gone on a long time, and some cultures see no reason to treat animals well. Religious beliefs that humankind is special and that animals do not have souls have sometimes been used to justify appalling exploitation and cruelty. But religious statements about other species tend to depend on the more general moral values of society and to change as we learn more about animal psychology. Some religious people think that God created the world and gave humans 'stewardship' over it, but this is not a belief that humanists can share, and they look elsewhere for reasons for caring about animals.

What have scientists and philosophers thought?

Scientists and philosophers have long argued about animal consciousness and suffering. In the 16th century Michel de Montaigne thought that animals were probably very like us: 'Why should we think that they have inner natural instincts different from anything we experience in ourselves?' But in the 17th century, some people, for example the philosopher René

Descartes, thought that animals could not feel pain and so we could do whatever we liked to them. A century later, the Scottish atheist philosopher David Hume wrote: 'We should be bound by the laws of humanity to give gentle usage to these creatures', which is probably a common view amongst humanists today. In 1789 the utilitarian Jeremy Bentham wrote of animals: 'The question is not, Can they reason? nor Can they talk? but Can they suffer?' Also in the 19th century, Charles Darwin's theory of evolution taught us how closely related to other animals we are, and how like us they can be. In the 20th century ecologists reminded us of the interdependence of species and the importance of conservation. People also first began to talk of 'animal rights' and 'speciesism', ideas pioneered by the atheist philosopher Peter Singer and still controversial; many people think that rights must be linked with duties and reciprocity, and it is difficult to see how animals can have duties or respect human rights.

Can animals suffer?

But whether animals can be said to have rights or not, concern for suffering does seem to be the key issue. We do not, on the whole, think it is possible to be cruel to plants because plants do not have nervous systems which can feel physical pain, or minds which can feel psychological pain (for example, fear). But we have all seen miserable or bored animals or heard them yelp with pain – it is difficult to believe seriously that they do not have feelings, and scientists have confirmed these everyday observations by methodical research. It is hard to be sure about the feelings of animals, but animal welfare scientists are beginning to work out more precisely what animals feel and what causes suffering. Research into the brains of animals shows that their brains and mental states are quite like ours and a great deal of testing on animals is done because we assume they are like us, physically and psychologically. But the more like us they are, the more they can suffer like us and the more they deserve our concern and respect.

What do humanists think?

Humanists would prefer not to cause unnecessary suffering to sentient beings, and discussion tends to focus on what is 'unnecessary suffering' and which animals are sentient. Most people think that fur coats are unnecessary luxuries and that the cruelty involved in farming or hunting animals for their fur cannot be justified. Many people also think that hunting and fishing for food or sport are cruel and unnecessary. Many people are willing to eat less meat, or no meat at all, in order to discourage what they see as the unnecessary cruelty involved in factory farming. (In Europe and the USA, 18 million pigs – intelligent animals – are kept in restrictive battery farm conditions.) Some people think that all killing of animals is wrong, whilst others argue that death cannot mean as much to

animals as it does to us, and so all that matters is rearing and killing them humanely. Some people oppose using animals for our entertainment, in zoos and circuses, or as pets (sometimes bred for characteristics that make life very difficult for the animal, for example flat faces that interfere with breathing). Humanists make use of reason and compassion when thinking about these questions, and will arrive at different conclusions, often depending on specific circumstances or situations.

The sharpest divisions of opinion are over the use of animals in experiments. Most people, whatever their religious beliefs, would probably agree that there are enough cosmetics and shampoos in the world to make the testing of new ones on animals unnecessary. But medical research is a different matter. Most of us would not want to use untested drugs or treatments, or to have new medicines tested on ourselves or other people. Many effective medicines and treatments have been discovered and refined in tests on animals, and many humanists would accept these tests as long as the benefits outweigh the costs – though this is not an easy calculation to make. It is also worth remembering that some research involving animals

is intended to improve animal welfare – for example, animals need medicines too. But it is certainly right to ensure that animal experiments are kept to a minimum and conducted as humanely as possible.

Most responsible human beings, and that includes most humanists, do not think that we should exploit or mistreat others just because they are different from us or we are bigger or cleverer than they are. Is this what we are doing when we mistreat animals? Most humanists simply do not want to be the kind of person who causes suffering or who tolerates cruelty, and for many that must include animals.

Further reading:

BHA briefings: *Thinking about Ethics, Environmental Issues, Genetic Engineering, 'Nature'*, Humanist Philosophers' Group, *What is Humanism?* (BHA, 2002), Peter Singer, *Animal Rights*, Mary Midgeley *Why Animals Matter*.

• By Marilyn Mason, with thanks to Dr Georgia Mason of Oxford University Department of Zoology, January 2002.

• The above information is from the British Humanist Association, see page 41 for their address details.

© *British Humanist Association (BHA)*

Why animal rights?

Animal rights is not about loving animals more than people, or putting their needs ahead of our own. It is about protecting animals from cruelty and unfair treatment – just as we would expect to be protected – and about trying not to do harm

What rights for animals?

Animals obviously do not need exactly the same rights as we do. For instance, the right to vote in elections would be worthless to a parrot. On the other hand, the right not to be tortured, or killed – except where the person who kills is acting in self-defence – is as valuable to animals as it is to us.

How do we use animals?

Millions of animals suffer pain and misery because of humans. We experiment on them in laboratories. We rear and slaughter

them for food. We take the skins off their backs and wear them as shoes, coats and sweaters. We hunt them for a jolly day out. We dump pets we no longer want. We imprison them in zoos and circuses to 'educate' and amuse ourselves. We pollute and destroy their natural environment.

Why care about animals?

Even today, some people think that animals are greatly inferior to humans and that they have no feelings or thoughts. This attitude can partly be blamed on the 18th-century French

scientist René Descartes, one of the first to experiment on animals. He argued that the squeals of pain from animals he cut open were mere noises from machines and not a sign of suffering.

Descartes still has his fans among some modern-day scientists. But it is now generally accepted that animals – just like humans – experience happiness, sadness, fear, physical pain, anger and boredom. We know that they usually enjoy the company of their own kind; that there is normally a close bond between mothers and their young;

that young animals enjoy and learn from play and that animals develop friendships.

Are people more intelligent?

Animals cannot play the clarinet (but then neither can most people). Nor have they invented weapons of mass destruction. But they can do some amazing things that we can't. For instance, can you swing through the trees like an orang utan? Or sniff out a bone 100 yards away in the bushes, like the average dog? Calling it 'instinct' doesn't make it less remarkable.

Deciding how to treat other creatures on the grounds of intelligence is all wrong. Logically, doing so would mean that the most intelligent people would have the most rights and that those who were born intellectually disabled, or who are damaged by illness or accident, would have the least rights. That wouldn't be fair or humane.

Can animals communicate?

Scientific tests have proved that gorillas and chimpanzees can learn how to communicate in human language. But we don't need more experiments to prove that animals can express their emotions to each other and to us. Anybody with pet animals will already know that they can show us when they are nervous, hungry or thirsty and that they remember people and places they haven't seen for months or even years.

Pain and suffering

Above all, we know that, just like us, animals feel pain and fear. Have you ever heard of an animal who can be cut by a knife, or burnt by a flame and not feel it? This is why they deserve our protection. As the 18th-century philosopher Jeremy Bentham pointed out: 'The question is not, can they reason? Nor, can they talk? But can they suffer?'

A lesson from history?

Similar excuses to those given for treating animals badly were once put forward to defend the exploitation of certain people. Slave owners argued that their slaves were unimportant and didn't deserve justice or equality because they were of a different race. African families were torn apart and hundreds of thousands of slaves suffered all kinds of abuse, humiliation and cruelty. They were worked to the point of collapse, even death. Is it so far-fetched to compare their fate with that of animals today?

Alice Walker, the well-known African-American writer, doesn't think so. She writes that: 'animals of the world exist for their own reason. They were not made for humans any more than black people were made for whites or women for men.'

One great family

It was not until 1948 that the world's nations joined together to issue the Universal Declaration of Human Rights which said that all people should have freedom and respect whatever their colour, gender, religion or race.

Those who believe in animal rights think that animals deserve similar protection. The fact that there is still a great deal of human pain and suffering in the world does not excuse animal abuse or mean that we should not try to help animals.

'It is clear that animals form lasting friendships, are frightened of being hunted, have a horror of dismemberment [having their limbs torn apart], wish they were back in the safety of their den, despair for their mates, look out for and protect their children whom they love . . . They feel throughout their lives, just as we do.'
Jeffrey Masson, *When Elephants Weep*.

What kind of future?

Animal Aid is working towards a future where animals are free from the suffering caused by exploitation.

Our vision of the future is one where medical research is carried out with humane methods and not by hurting animals; where animals are no longer imprisoned in factory farms to produce cheap meat; where better use is made of the world's food resources so that fewer people will go hungry; where wild animals are no longer hounded to death or shot for sport, or stripped of their skins and teeth and tusks; where we are entertained and amused by human skills and not by animals forced to perform for us; where endangered animals are secure and protected within nature reserves and not held captive in cages; where natural habitats such as tropical rain-forests are preserved for the animals and people who live there, rather than plundered and exploited for short term profits; and where all living creatures are treated with respect and compassion.

Living without cruelty

A change in attitude can make all the difference. By making informed choices about what we buy and eat and how we look after our health, we can all help to improve the way animals are treated. By choosing to become vegetarians, we show food producers that we want no part of a system that breeds and kills hundreds of millions of animals for food every year. We can also help to influence how manufacturers test their products by only buying those which have not involved any animal experiments. All new conventional drugs and medicines are tested on animals. But by doing everything we can to keep ourselves fit and healthy, and exploring 'alternative' remedies, we will only need drugs when it is really necessary. If you want to help replace human wrongs with animals rights, the first step is to get informed.

• The above information is from Animal Aid's web site which can be found at www.animalaid.org.uk Alternatively, see page 41 for their address details.

© Animal Aid

Animal welfare and animal rights

Information from the Countryside Alliance

What is meant by animal welfare and animal rights?

Let us begin by asking ourselves which of the following statements do we agree with the most?

A. Humans have complete domination over animals.

B. We have a duty to manage animals well and responsibly.

C. Animals have the same rights as humans

What is animal welfare?

Animal welfare is not a philosophy as such. It is a part of our culture, there are laws to protect animals, rules for the treatment of farm animals and many unwritten customs – all expressing the belief that animals should not be cruelly treated, and that people have a duty to look after them well. Many people who believe in animal welfare also believe that animals should be reared for food, killed if they are pests or be the quarry of sports such as fishing. There is no single definition of what is good or adequate animal welfare.

What is animal rights?

Animal rights is a philosophical viewpoint. Some people use the term 'animal rights' as a shorthand for better conditions for animals' but animal rights actually means much more than that. At the centre of the animal rights philosophy is the belief that animals must be included within the same system of morals that we apply to people. Therefore, a believer in animal rights would directly compare the needs of animals against the needs of people instead of putting the needs of animals second. He or she might decide that it is wrong to perform a medical procedure that sacrificed an animal, even if it saved a human life, because that would violate the animal's right to life. As with animal welfare,

COUNTRYSIDE ALLIANCE

individuals' beliefs about animal rights vary a lot. Some people believe that unless you give animals the same rights as people, you are a 'specialist', which is much like being a racist. The defining statement of the animal rights philosophy is Peter Singer's book *Animal Liberation*.

What is cruelty?

The 1911 Protection of Animals Act defines cruelty as the infliction of 'unnecessary' suffering. The definition of what constitutes 'unnecessary' suffering ultimately depends on your viewpoint as to what you perceive as unnecessary.

To some people, meat and dairy farming is unnecessary, therefore any of the inevitable suffering caused is also unnecessary; therefore farming is cruel. Whilst to others with a different set of values, livestock farming is a legitimate use of animals, and is not cruel as long as any suffering is minimised. Some people believe that keeping pets brings unnecessary suffering to the animals concerned.

Others feel that keeping pets is not cruel as long as the pet is looked after and cared for and is in good health.

However, it is clear that without the need for these animals, they would soon disappear from our lives altogether and probably cease to exist. We must also remember that the natural world is a world in which wild animals live and die without our intervention. The vast majority of wild animals in our hedgerows, fields, woodlands and wetlands die of disease, starvation and cold, without the veterinary assistance afforded to our domestic animals. Over-population in late spring and summer leads to a 'wastage' in winter when only the fittest will survive. Suffering will be involved but this is necessary to secure the survival of the species as a whole.

The Countryside Alliance believes that we have a duty to manage animals well and responsibly.

Key messages

There is no greater degree of suffering or cruelty through country pursuits than can be found in the natural environment People who take part in country pursuits recognise their responsibilities to their environment and the animals within it.

'Let us allow the dog to disappear from our brick and concrete jungles – from our firesides, from the leather nooses and chains by which we enslave it.'

John Bryant, former Chief Officer of the League Against Cruel Sports, from his book *Fettered Kingdoms*

- The above information is from the Countryside Alliance's web site which can be found at www.countryside-alliance.org Alternatively, see page 41 for their address details.

© Countryside Alliance

Animal cruelty culture

Children tainted by our animal cruelty culture. Many youngsters admit they abuse pets just for fun, says shock RSPCA report. By James Chapman, Science Correspondent

Half of all children over ten have had first-hand experience of animal cruelty, according to shocking figures from the RSPCA.

The youngsters have either seen an adult do something that caused pain or suffering to an animal – or done it themselves.

'It ranged from kicking cats out of anger to beating animals for fun,' the charity's Ros Varnes said last night.

The figures badly damage Britain's claim to be a nation of animal lovers and reveal a big increase in the number of abandoned, abused and neglected pets.

The RSPCA is now receiving a call for help every 19 seconds and experienced officers used to dealing with abuse have been shocked by the torment inflicted on some family pets.

Worryingly, teenagers were guilty of some of the most cruel attacks. It was research commissioned to understand their behaviour that revealed how many have been involved in animal abuse.

Experts at Manchester Metropolitan University interviewed 1,000 ten to 16-year-olds and concluded that cruelty to animals was 'deep-rooted' in society from childhood.

The research also suggested that many Britons have a 'throwaway' attitude to family pets, said Mrs Varnes.

'In our consumerist culture it seems that people are increasingly willing just to discard animals once they realise the commitment and time that's involved in looking after them,' she added;

'A great many people in this country still have an abiding respect and love for animals. But there is a significant minority who do not and we have to step up our efforts to change that.' Heather Piper, from the Institute of Education at Manchester, who carried out the study of children's attitudes for the

RSPCA, said: 'A lot of the children were retaliating against the animals because they had bitten them or torn their clothes.

'Or it may have been jealousy because the animal was receiving a lot of attention.'

She added that a number of children admitted they hurt animals for fun.

'In our consumerist culture it seems that people are increasingly willing just to discard animals once they realise the commitment and time that's involved in looking after them'

Dr Mike Johnson, another member of the research team, said animal abuse is found across society.

He claimed that Prince Charles's support for foxhunting set a bad example. He said one of the children interviewed had said: 'Why should it be OK for him to chase foxes on horses and not for us to chase cats?'

The RSPCA's figures revealed that inspectors rescued 193,280 animals last year – a 16 per cent increased on 1999. Persecutions for harming animals jumped by nine per cent.

The RSPCA highlighted the case of a jealous husband jailed for three months for bludgeoning his wife's cat to death in a violent rage.

Rupert Ford, 32, from Redruth, Cornwall, was also banned from keeping animals for life. A court heard he had killed Rufus, a Siamese cross, with a hammer after finding his wife in a pub with her ex-boyfriend.

RSPCA inspector Paul Kempson said: 'This was a sickening and disturbing case in which a man took out his anger on a defenceless animal in the most violent way possible.'

A teenager who twice hurled a puppy off a 70ft railway bridge was jailed for six months and banned from keeping any animals for 25 years.

Obi a spaniel cross, had a fractured skull and some neurological damage after plunging from the bridge between Ashington and Stakeford, Northumberland.

The RSPCA is now planning to step up its schools education programme.

Different views

Information from the Association of the British Pharmaceutical Industry (ABPI)

Some people opposed to the use of animals in research take an absolute stance for moral reasons and say that no animals should ever be used in research, regardless of the benefits that research may bring. For other campaigners the choice is easier, as they believe that information from animals studies is of no value in human medicine – a view that is at odds with mainstream medical and scientific opinion throughout the world.

Other people argue that in a society which consumes hundreds of millions of animals a year as food, and in which millions more animals are destroyed because they are seen as pests or vermin, it's illogical to object to their use in medical research, an area that involves far fewer animals and can do so much good.

Probably the majority position is that in a humane society, animals should not be subjected to needless distress, but the needs of humans take precedence.

The following statements put different views about animal research that may be helpful in school discussions.

Animal research is not needed to make new medicines . . .
Animal research has been and continues to be essential for the development of new medicines . . .

Regardless of the benefits, animal research is morally wrong. There is no justification . . .
Nobody wants to use animals for research but it would be much worse to let people be ill, in pain or die unnecessarily . . .

Animals are cruelly treated in UK laboratories. Scientists only care about their research, not the animals . . .
Most scientists care a great deal about
the animals they use and animal research is strictly controlled by law . . .

Animal research does not help in the development of medicines for people. Animals are too biologically dissimilar to give useful information about the effects of medicines in people. Whatever your moral position, animals tell you about animals, not people . . .
Animals' and people's bodies are not exactly the same but the similarities are enormous compared to the differences. Provided the research is well designed and conducted, animals give essential guidance about the effects of medicines in people . . .

We would not need research if people took better care of themselves. Prevention is better than cure . . .
Prevention is always better than cure. We should prevent illness where we can, and treat it where we cannot . . .

We can find out all we need to know from careful observation of patients and the identification of factors which lead to illness, along with increased use of computers and cell culture tests . . .
Computer and test-tube research provides some of the necessary information. In addition, scientists need to study the effects of a medicine in carefully designed animal studies. Only then could doctors justify testing medicines in people . . .

Animal research gives misleading information, making medicines look safe when they are not. That is why medicines have unexpected side-effects . . .
Animal research gives scientists a good indication of what to expect in patients so that the human studies can be conducted safely. But even years of these studies involving thousands of patients cannot guarantee that a medicine is safe for everyone . . .

If scientists really cared about using alternatives, they would have already replaced all animal experiments . . .
Wherever non-animal methods give the necessary information, they are used. The contribution of these methods is increasing all the time but it will be a long time, if ever, before it will be possible to mimic all the functions of a complete living body by computer or in the test-tube . . .

• The above information is an extract from the Association of the British Pharmaceutical Industry's (ABPI) web site which can be found at www.abpi.org.uk

Alternatively, see page 41 for their postal address details.

Introduction to animal experiments

Information from the British Union for the Abolition of Vivisection (BUAV)

In 1999 2.57 million living animals were used in experimental procedures in Great Britain, of which two-thirds were not given any anaesthetic.[1]

These experiments were performed in three main areas of research: to increase scientific knowledge, to develop new products and to test the safety of new products and their ingredients.

Because of the pain and suffering involved in such experiments, legislation requires each procedure to be licensed. For example, animals may be electrocuted, deprived of food and water, surgically mutilated, exposed to radiation, burned and scalded, deliberately wounded, exposed to nerve gas, infected with deadly diseases and poisoned with products as varied as household cleaners, weed killers and drugs.

What animals are used?

All kinds of animals are used, including horses, donkeys, pigs, sheep, hamsters, and frogs. These are only the figures for 1999 in Britain. World-wide, it is estimated that over a hundred million animals are used in similar experiments each year.

Where do they come from?

(i) Commercial breeding
The majority of animals are purpose-bred and supplied by specialist companies. Economic considerations are a major factor in the use of laboratory animals. A laboratory mouse costs approximately £1.40, a cat about £100 and a beagle dog around £800. Animals are bred for particular qualities relevant to research needs. For example, rabbits are relatively cheap and docile and their large eyes, which cannot produce tears, make them popular for irritancy tests, as they are unable to 'cry' away, naturally, any product dripped into the eye.[2]

(ii) Pet stealing
There has been a history of concern about pet stealing as a source of supply for laboratories. Certainly there are many examples of non-purpose-bred animals being used in experiments. In 1989 the BUAV obtained proof that ex-racing greyhounds were being sent for vivisection after they retired from the track.[3] From 1990 all laboratories have had to buy their animals from breeding establishments and suppliers licensed by the Home Office.

(iii) Wild animals
Some animals are trapped in the wild. The methods used are cruel and indiscriminate and a threat to some endangered species. Once captured many animals that are considered unsuitable for research are killed needlessly. Others die from disease, stress and inadequate care during transport. The BUAV estimates that 80% of primates caught in the wild will die before reaching the laboratory.

Where do they go?

All premises conducting animal experiments have to hold a licence granted by the Home Office. The following percentages are from the total number of procedures started in 1998. They were carried out by:

(i) Commercial companies (41.5%) – who run contract testing laboratories involved in testing new products such as drugs and cosmetics.

(ii) Universities / medical schools (35.2%) – who have their own labs for educational and research purposes. They are also commissioned to do research by external bodies such as commercial companies and medical charities.

(iii) Government Departments/ public health labs/NHS hospitals (7%) – this figure includes work done in public health labs and NHS hospitals. They have their own laboratories and research centres, for example, military research using animals is carried out at Porton Down Laboratories, on behalf of the

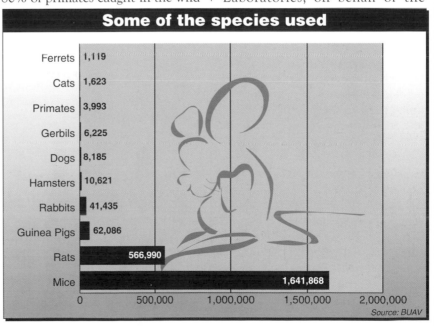

Some of the species used

Species	Number
Ferrets	1,119
Cats	1,623
Primates	3,993
Gerbils	6,225
Dogs	8,185
Hamsters	10,621
Rabbits	41,435
Guinea Pigs	62,086
Rats	566,990
Mice	1,641,868

Source: BUAV

Ministry of Defence. The Ministry of Agriculture, Fisheries and Food has labs for research such as developing new breeds of farm animals and for testing new agricultural chemicals.

(iv) Charities/non-profit organisations (4.5%) – may have their own labs and also commission research projects in universities. This research is not included in the above figure.

(v) Other public bodies (11.8%)

Why are animal experiments performed?

Scientists use animals as 'models' of human beings. In reality, the difference between species can vary greatly, casting doubt over the reliability of the results of animal tests. Present morality permits the infliction of pain and suffering on animals that would be considered unthinkable for humans.

(i) Medical and veterinary Research makes up a large proportion of all experiments on animals and involves a wide range of procedures. Animals are used in medical training as 'living models' of how the body works, or as 'tools' for learning practical skills.

Animals are used to see how their body reacts to disease, infection, drugs and new surgical techniques. Certain types of animals are favoured for different types of research, for example, mice are used for cancer research, dogs for the development of surgical techniques such as transplant surgery, cats for psychological experiments and primates for vaccine research.

(ii) Drug research is the major area of medical research. Again, used as models for the human condition, animals are infected with diseases and then dosed with drugs to assess their effectiveness, toxicity and possible side-effects. The most well-known toxicity test around the world is the LD50 (Lethal Dose 50%) in which animals, most often rats, mice, or rabbits, are deliberately poisoned to death, in order to determine the single dose needed to kill 50% of the animals used.[4,5] Groups of animals are given the test substance at increased dose levels, either by force feeding, injection, application to the

skin or inhalation and observed for up to 14 days. Common signs of poisoning are vomiting, distress, tremors, diarrhoea, convulsions and bleeding.

Many scientists have now condemned the LD50 test as unreliable and recognise that the results have little relevance to the human condition. Thanks to a challenge by the BUAV, the UK government has now banned the LD50 oral toxicity test. However, it is still widely used world-wide.

(iii) Household product tests – products such as bleach, washing powder and washing-up liquid are also tested on animals using, for example, the LD50 and irritancy tests.

The Draize Test – this test involves a substance being dripped into one eye of a rabbit. The eye is then examined for signs of bleeding, ulceration, redness, swelling and discharge over a period of several days. The albino rabbit is traditionally used because it is cheap, docile, readily available and has large eyes for assessing test results.

Skin Irritancy Tests – this test involves a substance being applied to the shaved skin of rabbits or rodents. The area is then observed for signs of redness, inflammation, swelling and cracking, while the animals are held immobile in restraining devices, to prevent them from licking the test area.

(iv) Environmental pollutants – using test procedures such as the LD50, skin irritancy and long term toxicity tests, products such as pesticides, herbicides and industrial chemicals are tested on animals to assess their safety and potential toxicity to the environment and to human health.

Ultimately, say the scientists, it is a choice between a man or a mouse. Whose survival is more important? The real choice, however, is between good science and bad science

---

(v) Agricultural experiments – modern factory farming techniques produce problems of disease and infection and animals are used to develop new drugs to treat these resulting conditions. These experiments are often motivated by the need to increase productivity and profit, rather than concern for animal welfare. Animals are also used in breeding programmes aimed at producing new strains of animal, capable of producing more food, more quickly.

(vi) Warfare and space research – There is little information about this research, as it is protected by Government secrecy laws. However, we do know that animals such as rodents, pigs, dogs and sheep are gassed, burned and injured in experiments to develop and test biological weapons, riot and nerve gases and ballistics. In space research, animals such as dogs and monkeys have been sent into space with electrodes planted in their brains and upon return to earth, have been killed for dissection and autopsy. There is little direct evidence of space research in Britain. Most is carried out in the United States and former Soviet Union.

(vii) Psychology experiments – In the hope of improving our understanding of how the human brain functions and affects human behaviour, scientists use animals in procedures which include starvation, electrocution, water deprivation, separation of young animals from their mother, solitary confinement and rearing in complete darkness.

Do animal experiments work?

Experiments on animals are unreliable because they tell us about animals, not people. For example, aspirin causes birth defects in rats and mice, but not in humans, while penicillin, which is a life saver in humans, is poisonous to guinea pigs.

Leading drug company Ciba Geigy has admitted that 95% of substances passed 'safe' by animal tests are rejected immediately in human studies.

Some tests are designed in such a way that the results are clearly dubious, long before the test is carried out. For example, in one poisoning test, rats were dosed with the human equivalent of 4lbs of lipstick. Eventually, one rat died, not from poisoning, but from intestinal obstruction.

Animals are usually selected on the grounds of convenience and cost, the vast majority of animals used being mice and rats, and not on the basis of their 'human similarities'. The results produced by animal experiments are both crude and unreliable. They provide no guarantee that a product will be safe or effective for humans.

Are animal experiments cruel?

Because the animals will feel pain, discomfort and stress, the experiments have to be licensed under the Animals (Scientific Procedures) Act 1986. However, the Act only attempts to prevent 'unnecessary' suffering. In reality, this means very little, as many of the procedures listed above are regularly carried out without any anaesthetic.

Are they morally justifiable?

Although animals differ from humans in important ways, there are also similarities. They can clearly feel physical pain and, in varying capacities, also experience fear, stress, pleasure and boredom. It is with this knowledge, and indeed because of it, that scientists perform animal experiments.

Is it morally justifiable to inflict such suffering on another living creature? Scientists would argue that it is, because of the potential benefits to human beings. But, if this is so, why should we not also experiment on human beings, who will yield much more relevant results? That we do not extend our morality to other species can only be explained in terms of simple prejudice. There is no other rational explanation.

Ultimately, say the scientists, it is a choice between a man or a mouse. Whose survival is more important? The real choice, however, is between good science and bad science. Whether to continue to use cruel and unreliable animal tests, or to use other more reliable, humane methods of direct relevance to people.

What are the alternatives?

Firstly, we must consider whether the test is really necessary. Many

experiments are performed merely to satisfy academic curiosity, to fulfil a bureaucratic demand or because results of similar tests have been kept secret. A huge number relate to the production of products which are just minor variations of those already available (i.e. me-too drugs). Non-animal research techniques are also overlooked because a company may claim that they are inconvenient or more expensive compared to animal tests.

A wide variety of useful research techniques, which do not use animals, already exist and have further potential for development, if funding were to be diverted from animal research. These methods include using human cell and tissue cultures, test-tube techniques and sophisticated computer models. Clinical studies involving human patients are also very important. People who are ill can be observed very closely, to locate the cause and possible treatment. New drugs developed using test-tube techniques can also be administered in small quantities to observe the effects. This is already what happens after animal tests and it is the most crucial stage of research.

Many forms of illness have been treated successfully for many years using methods developed without animal testing. These include Herbalism, Acupuncture, Osteopathy, Homeopathy and Chiropractice.

Perhaps most important of all, much more could be done to prevent illness and disease. Studies of human populations can reveal the causes of ill health. This was how it was established that smoking causes lung cancer. Cancer and heart disease are the major killers in Britain, yet there is considerable evidence to show that they are largely preventable. Greater emphasis on prevention could save many thousands of lives each year.

Conclusion

Animal experiments are widely used in Britain and many other countries. As a result, millions of animals suffer great pain and misery. The morality of such experiments must be questioned. So too must the relevance and the reliability of the results. More resources should be directed towards epidemiological (population) studies and developing alternative non-animal methods of research.

References

1 Home Office, *Statistics of Scientific Procedures on Living Animals Great Britain*, 1999. The Stationery Office.

2 Sharpe R., (1988), *The Cruel Deception*. Thorsons Publishing Group.

3 McIvor, S., Race Against Death (*Liberator*, BUAV, Summer 1989).

4 Kondo, A. et al, (1996), *British J. of Cancer* 73(10): 1166-70.

5 Chamorro, G. et al, (1994), *Archives of Medical Research* 25(4): 441-6.

Popular misunderstandings

Information from Huntingdon Life Sciences

Myth – 'The use of animals in biomedical research is unnecessary because equivalent information can be obtained by alternative methods'

Those who would seek to abolish animal research often claim that the use of animals in biomedical research is unnecessary because information can be obtained by alternative methods, such as test tubes and computers.

What is often not realised is that scientists have strong ethical, economic and legal obligations to use animals in research only when absolutely necessary. A lot of effort goes into trying to reduce the numbers of animals used, and trying to develop new methods to replace animals. As a result, the number of laboratory animals used annually in this country has almost halved in the last 20 years.

Non-animal methods – tissue culture, computer modelling, studies of patients and populations – are very widely used. In fact, only about five pence in every pound spent on medical research goes on animal studies. The word alternatives, often used to describe these non-animal methods, can lead to confusion because these methods are generally used alongside animal studies, not instead of them. All these techniques have their place, and it is rarely possible to substitute one for another.

There are stages in any research programme when it is not enough to know how individual molecules, cells or tissues behave. The living body is much more than just a collection of these parts, and we need to understand how they interact, how they are controlled. There are ethical limits to the experiments that we can perform in people, so the only alternative is to use the most suitable animal to study a particular disease or biological function.

It is illegal to expose patients to new medicines without being confident that they are likely to benefit and not be seriously harmed. Treat-

Huntingdon Life Sciences
Working for a better future

ments must, therefore, be tested first in animals to establish their probable effectiveness and safety. They are then tested on human volunteers. The process is not perfect but testing in whole animals is by far the best way to protect people.

For example, it is difficult to even imagine what range of test-tube techniques or the complexity of computer systems that would be necessary to mimic the amazing events that occur during the development and birth of a new baby. With present-day technology, and even in the foreseeable future, this is simply not possible. By contrast, appropriate whole animal tests can detect potentially harmful effects of new treatments on foetal development and other events during pregnancy. Thus another thalidomide disaster is most unlikely.

No one wants to use animals unnecessarily or to cause them unnecessary suffering. The guiding principles in animal research today are called the Three Rs:

- Refinement, to make sure animals suffer as little as possible
- Reduction, to minimise the number of animals used
- Replacement, to replace animal procedures with non-animal techniques wherever possible.

Myth – 'The welfare of animals in research is secretive and is not regulated'

All animals involved in scientific research are very closely regulated. The most important document governing this work is the Animals (Scientific Procedures) Act 1986, which includes a benefit analysis that must be applied before any research project involving animals can proceed. Thus the costs, in terms of potential animal suffering, must be weighed against the potential benefits of the research. The Act requires that animal procedures:

- take place in designated premises (which must obtain a certificate of designation)
- form part of an approved programme of work (which must obtain a project licence)
- are conducted by competent persons (who must obtain a personal licence)

    Licences are only granted if:

- the potential results are important enough to justify the use of animals (the benefit analysis)
- the research cannot be done using non-animal methods
- the minimum number of animals will be used
- dogs, cats or primates are only used when absolutely necessary
- any discomfort or suffering is kept to a minimum by appropriate use of anaesthetics or pain killers
- researchers and technicians conducting procedures have the necessary training, skills and experience
- research premises have the necessary facilities to look after the animals properly (laid down in a Home Office Code of Practice).

To ensure that all animal-based research is done according to these controls, the Home Office employs a team of inspectors, who are all qualified vets or doctors. On average, they visit each research establishment eight times a year usually without prior notice. In addition, at each establishment a vet must be on call at all times.

Myth – 'Animals cannot be compared to humans, therefore it is pointless using animals in experiments'

All mammals are descended from common ancestors, and one result of this is that humans are biologically very similar to other mammals. All mammals, including humans, have the same organs – heart, lungs, kidneys, liver etc. – performing the same functions and controlled by the same mechanisms, via the blood stream and nervous system.

Of course there are minor differences, but these are far outweighed by the remarkable similarities. The differences can give important clues about diseases and how they might be treated.

Vitamins and hormones identified by animal experiments were found to have similar functions in people. The following animal hormones have all been used successfully in human patients:

- insulin from the pancreas of pigs or cows
- thyrotropin from cows' pituitaries
- calcitonin from the parathyroid gland of salmon
- adrenocorticotrophic hormone from pituitaries of farm animals
- oxytocin and vasopressin from pig posterior pituitary glands.

No one will claim that animals are identical to humans but in the struggle to find new cures and better treatments, animals remain the closest model to human beings.

Myth – 'Animal testing is unreliable, because drugs have different effects in people and animals. Therefore drugs that are passed as safe in animals are found to have serious side-effects in people.'

During the development of new chemical entities, medicines must pass extensive screening by test-tube methods before they are allowed to be exposed to animals. These tests give valuable information about how the drug reacts in the living body, and often show up previously unpredicted side-effects. For instance, the route of administration

---

No one wants to use animals unnecessarily or to cause them unnecessary suffering

---

is important: a drug given by mouth may be altered by digestion, becoming less effective or more toxic. This is the sort of problem that will not be apparent from test-tube results, but will only show up in a living body.

The animal tests are designed to reveal potentially undesirable effects such as liver damage, raised blood pressure, nerve damage, or damage to the foetus. The results of the animal studies will give a strong indication of what the effects in people are likely to be. It is obviously important, and is required by law, to find out about potential problems before drugs are given to human volunteers and patients in clinical trials.

Human clinical trials will involve testing a drug on 3-5,000 human volunteers and patients. If a side-effect affecting say 1 in 10,000 patients does occur, this could only show up after the product is on the market – it is unlikely that any such problem could have been spotted before. This does not invalidate the research data gained from the work with animals.

The number of drugs withdrawn from the market is also consistently overstated by animal rights activists, who often refer to 'an endless list'. In fact, of the 2,000 types of drug on the market, less than 40 have been withdrawn in the UK, US, France or Germany. This indicates a success rate of at least 98% for drug testing procedures. In fact, only 10 of these drugs have been withdrawn in all four countries.

• The above information is from Huntingdon Life Sciences' web site which can be found at www.huntingdon.com/index.html

© *Huntingdon Life Sciences*

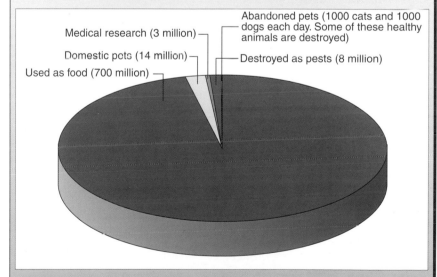

The use of animals by society

The pie chart below shows the numbers of animals used in the UK in one year. The major areas are for food, as companion animals (pets), in medical research and those destroyed as pests (mostly rats and mice) and those cats and dogs abandoned and destroyed by animal welfare organisations.

Abandoned pets (1000 cats and 1000 dogs each day. Some of these healthy animals are destroyed)

Medical research (3 million)

Domestic pets (14 million)

Used as food (700 million)

Destroyed as pests (8 million)

We can see from the chart that the vast majority, some 97%, of animals are slaughtered and consumed as food. That is approximately 12 animals for every person in the UK every year. In order to investigate diseases, develop and test new medicines and other therapies the biomedical research community uses a very small fraction, about 0.36%, of the animals used in the UK.

Source: Biomedical Research Education Trust

The debate about animal experiments

Information from Uncaged Campaigns

Introduction

The debate about animal experiments has two principle components: does animal experimentation benefit human beings, and can it ever be morally justified even if it does?

Both these issues are complex but neither are so complex that clear conclusions cannot be drawn. Uncaged are not afraid of the debate – because we are sure that a rational examination of the issues must support our view – and so we encourage you to examine the arguments of our opponents. The web site of the Research Defence Society (RDS), the main organisation defending animal experiments, is found at www.rds-online.org.uk. Check it out.

Below we try to evaluate all the arguments. We commence with the first part of the debate.

Animal experiments: vital or dangerous?

The evidence for . . .

Supporters of animal experiments claim that they are vital to medical progress and that human lives have been and continue to be saved by them. They claim that major advances in medical techniques and therapies depend on information gained from experiments in animals and they point to many examples of apparently beneficial experiments. The evidence they produce certainly has a superficial plausibility: experiments on animals that appear to show results relevant to human illnesses can certainly be identified. Intuition suggests that many animals have both differences from and similarities with human beings, and surely those similarities must be useful. When examples of humans and animals responding to substances in similar ways, or of human treatments inspired by results in animals are produced, the scientific

value of animal experiments appears to be confirmed. (The RDS web site features very many such examples, with extensive references.) The reality of the situation is rather more complex.

Firstly, experiments which provide useless or irrelevant information are usually not published (in fact the majority of research goes unpublished), and those which lead to no useful conclusions are forgotten. 'Positive' results are easy to identify, but the failure of animal experiments to provide truly effective cures or treatments for thousands of illnesses must also be figured into the equation. Ignoring negative results produces the illusion that animal research has a high success rate. Logically, out of countless millions of experiments conducted over the last hundred-and-fifty years, some must 'succeed' but if this proportion is very low the whole methodology must be questioned.

> *It is hard for lay-people to assess arguments about science, and it is harder still when the debate is as polarised as the debate about animal experiments*

Secondly, the existence of animal research related to an illness or treatment does not prove that it was essential to the development of

that treatment or that it was even useful. All drugs and treatments must, by law, be tested on animals: defenders of vivisection can therefore always find examples which appear to support their claims, but these examples do not prove the necessity for experiments. We know that no treatment can be considered safe or effective until it has been tried in human patients: conversely we can never know that any animal procedure will produce results replicable in humans. Therefore it appears absurd to suggest that they are essential to the development of treatments.

Medical scientists and doctors draw on a range of techniques in developing new treatments, including logic and observation of patients in clinical practice. When we examine the history of medical science we find that it is these techniques and skills which have been truly essential. The responses of human beings to substances and diseases are obviously far more useful to doctors than those of different animal species, and far less likely to be misleading. Unsurprisingly then, the advances often alleged to have been derived from animal research invariably owe very much to the study of human beings. Indeed, animal experiments have sometimes produced results so misleading that advances have been delayed by years, as we detail later.

One also notices, in examining the examples identified by defenders of animal experiments, that many are very old indeed. When examining the footnotes on the RDS homepage one can easily find research papers dating back fifty years or more, and almost none later than 1980. Even if animal experiments had a significant role many years ago, that hardly proves that they are essential now. This view is also supported by the fact that the advances claimed in recent years are rather less impressive than those claimed for many years ago. One can certainly debate the role of animals (and we do) in the development of penicillin and the treatment of diabetes, but these advances are immeasurably more significant than improved immunosuppressant and leukaemia drugs, welcome as these are.

Even the RDS cannot provide evidence that the vastly increased numbers and sophistication of animal experiments in recent years have resulted in vastly greater benefits to human beings. If animal experiments are methodologically-sound and effective, they should have become more productive as our skills and knowledge have increased. They have not. Sadly, the experimenters cannot claim that this is because the major battles against illness have been won. Cures for AIDS, cancer, malaria and Alzheimer's disease have been promised for a long time – and still are – but literally millions of animal experiments over many decades have demonstrably failed to provide them so far.

It is hard for lay-people to assess arguments about science, and it is harder still when the debate is as polarised as the debate about animal experiments. By a process of selection and presentation historical data can be used to prove almost anything. A critical approach is, therefore, essential to this argument. The RDS's interpretation of history is not the only one available, and we will soon be publishing detailed responses to some of their specific claims. Meanwhile, compare their arguments with ours, and make up your own mind.

Animal experiments: the case against
Even a brief examination of the history of medical science reveals an abundance of evidence that animal experiments have caused human suffering. Examples of misleading results, dangerous therapies and numerous false dawns are easily found, and we list just a handful below. What are impossible to list are the treatments that failed on animals but which may have been effective in human beings. The existence of such evidence is hardly surprising: the fact is that the physiological differences between animals and humans make it impossible to predict the human response from an animal experiment. Experimenters may be able to identify physiological processes common to humans and some animals prior to an experiment but even very small differences in other body processes can and do affect the results obtained, with the kind of results described below.

- The development of the polio vaccine clearly demonstrates the harmfulness of animal research. J. Paul's *History of Poliomyelitis* (1971, New Haven: Yale University Press) details how research on rhesus monkeys seriously misled researchers for some 25 years because scientists subscribed to the rhesus monkey model of polio (nose as portal of entry for the virus) rather than the human evidence which indicated that the virus entered through the intestinal tract. It is impossible to ascertain how many lives were lost because of these animal experiments.

- Animal experiments also mislead us about the dangers of smoking. By the early 1960s, epidemiologists discerned a strong correlation between lung cancer and smoking. Yet because of the failure to induce lung cancer in experiments on animals, the link was considered seriously doubtful, and delayed the placement of health warnings on tobacco products (E. Northrup, *Science Looks at Smoking*, New York: Conard-McCann, 1957, p.133). Given that smoking is now the principle cause of premature death in the UK, the human death toll exacted by these animal experiments must be significant (Jacobson, Bobbie, et al, ed. *The Nation's Health – A Strategy for the 1990s*, King Edward's Hospital Fund for London, 1991, p.30).

- Thalidomide, Opren, FIAU and Eraldin were all drugs that caused serious (often fatal) side-effects in humans which were not foreseen by animal experiments. As recently as December 1997 the diabetic drug troglitazone was withdrawn from sale after only three months. It had caused 130 cases of liver failure and 6 deaths, yet had passed all animal tests.

• The above information is an extract from the Uncaged Campaigns web site which can be found at www.uncaged.co.uk Alternatively, see page 41 for their address details.

© Uncaged Campaigns

The hope, the challenge, the people

Perspectives on animal research

RDS

The people who agreed to be interviewed and photographed for a new RDS publication to be launched on 15 January 2002 are convinced that the use of animals in medical research is essential. They also agree that alternative methods should be sought to replace animal research and testing and that, until these are available, the numbers of animals used should be minimised and the experimental procedures refined to minimise any distress or suffering.

This is what they say in the publication, called *The Hope, the Challenge, the People*:

Laura, 16, has cystic fibrosis and may not reach her 30th birthday:

'I don't know what "normal" is. To control my cystic fibrosis and diabetes, I take between 50 and 70 tablets, plus two insulin injections and two nebulised drugs, every day. Those medicines have all been tested on animals so I'm very grateful to the people and the animals. Without them, I'd be dead.'

Donald has seen great strides in medicine during his 30-year career as a GP:

'When people ask me whether research on live animals is relevant, I tell them that there's a huge overlap between the medicines doctors prescribe for humans and those vets administer to animals. There are numerous diseases which animals and people both get, although they are different from species to species. Fortunately, we don't normally catch diseases from animals or vice versa.'

Paul is a surgeon pioneering new surgical transplant techniques through research on rats:

'I'm about to investigate how transplanted tissue in the intestines reacts to food and toxins. Does the grafted tissue behave as part of the recipient's system and mimic its responses, or does the donated material bring its own immune responses with it? Could we transfer food allergies or sensitivities between donor and recipient? No non-animal model can answer these questions because we need to study what happens outside the bowel, in the recipient's liver and immune system as well.'

Nancy leads a research team looking for new treatments for stroke and head injury:

'I don't like using animals. I use them because seeing people with devastating illnesses is even worse. The day when we don't need to use animals, I will be absolutely delighted. Until that day comes, I have absolutely no doubt that the animal research must continue'

Matt, a vet, is responsible for the welfare of animals used in a medical research programme:

'As a Named Veterinary Surgeon for a major company, I am the advocate for the animal and I am answerable ultimately to the Royal College of Veterinary Surgeons. That gives me a degree of independence from the company that employs me. I am here for the health and welfare of the animals.'

The publication also includes a timeline of major medical milestones over the last century, an introduction to the issue and further information about RDS. Copies are available from the RDS office, along with two subsidiary publications that present up-to-date information in a lively and accessible way – *Facts and figures on animal research in Great Britain* and *Animals in medical research: a guide to the information available*. Together, these publications provide useful information for schools, the media, politicians and civil servants: indeed anyone who wants to know more about the use of animals in medical research.

• The above information about *The Hope, the Challenge, the People*, an RDS publication, is from the Research Defence Society's (RDS) web site which can be found at w w w . r d s - o n l i n e . o r g . u k Alternatively, see page 41 for their address details.

Animal testing is a disaster

Thousands of people have been injured or killed by drugs that were found to be safe for other species

By Jerome Burne

What do you feel is more important – the life of your child or the life of a few rats? Such stark contrasts are common currency in the heavily polarised debate about experiments on animals. On the one side the misguided sentimentality of the animal rights campaigners, on the other side the tireless pursuit of human happiness and health by the researchers.

But since those wide-eyed activists have put animals' rights somewhere on the election agenda, you may be interested to know that there is a totally hard-headed and rational case to be made for saying that animal experimentation has been a scientific and medical disaster. That far from saving lives, it has caused injury and death to thousands and that time and again it has led both researchers and legislators into a blind alley.

But surely, you cry, we need animal experiments to discover how safe new drugs are before we give them to humans? Well, the combination of fenfluramine and dexfenfluramine, touted as the answer to a dieter's prayer a few years ago, was extensively tested on animals and found to be very safe. Unfortunately it caused heart valve abnormalities in humans. Or how about the arthritis drug Opren? Tests on monkeys found no problems but it killed 61 people before it was withdrawn. And as for having to choose between rats and your child, Cylert, given to children with attention deficit hyperactive disorder, was fine for animals but caused liver failure in 13 children.

The problem is not a new one, in fact it is blindingly obvious – animals are not the same as humans, so drugs that affect them in one way may well affect us differently.

Now this is usually presented as a solvable problem by researchers. We can get an idea of the mechanism from animals and then fine-tune with humans, they say, but it doesn't work like that. Species, even those that seem closely related, may function quite differently at a molecular level, and there is no way of predicting what the differences will be.

Rats and mice, for instance, look pretty alike to us, but when it comes to something as basic as whether a chemical causes cancer or not, the results may be totally contradictory. Out of 392 chemicals tested for carcinogenic effects at the American National Institute of Environmental Health Sciences, 96 were positive in the rat and negative in the mouse or vice versa. So which of those are harmful to humans? The institute can't say.

For 30 years they fed high doses of a range of new chemicals to animals to discover if they caused cancer or other damage. The results are recorded in blue books that take up 10 feet of shelving in the institute. But ask how many of the substances might produce tumours in humans at normal levels and no one knows. So what about the ones that didn't harm rodents, how many of them might harm humans? They don't know that either.

The lack of predictable differences between animal and human reactions is something that has bedevilled Aids research. Aids is a high profile disease with a lot of research money available, so it surely makes sense to ignore ethical objections and use chimpanzees. It is

> *The problem is not a new one, in fact it is blindingly obvious – animals are not the same as humans*

surely precisely because their genome is identical to ours, give or take a few percentage points, that they should yield more accurate results than rodents.

Well, no, actually. Out of approximately 100 chimps infected with HIV over a 10-year period only two have become sick. Chimp vaccine trials have proved unreliable too because they don't show the antibody or cell-mediated response to HIV that humans do. Animal experimentation has played only a small role in developing drug treatments to the greatest plague of our time.

And the list could go on. There are drugs that have been held back because they caused dangerous reaction in animals, such as beta blockers and valium, but then turned out to be safe for humans. Legislation to halt the use of asbestos was held up for years because it didn't cause cancer in animals, while the carcinogen benzene continued to be used long after clinicians were worried because it didn't cause leukaemia in mice.

All these examples, and many more, have been written up in the specialist journals but until last year they had been scattered. Then a man called Ray Greek, an American medical doctor who specialised in the highly technical field of anaesthesia, collected them in a book called *Sacred Cows and Golden Geese*. He gave a talk in London about it last night.

So was this scientific, rational contribution to the debate about animal experiments warmly welcomed, so medical research could be improved? Supporters of animal experiments are always calling for more public discussion and education.

Of course not. It was ignored.

• Jerome Burne is editor of the monthly newsletter *Medicine Today*.

Animals in medicines research

Questions and answers

What law protects animals used in research?

UK research involving laboratory animals is conducted under the Animals (Scientific Procedures) Act 1986, widely recognised as the most comprehensive law of its kind in the world. Its aim is to balance the legitimate needs of research with the welfare of animals. The law has many provisions. All the research, including a detailed explanation of its purpose, the likely effects on the animals and why the research cannot be done in other ways, must be approved in advance by the Home Office – the government department that oversees the Act.

What animals do you use and how can they help?

More than 80 per cent of animals used in UK medicines research are rodents. Because of the biological similarities between humans and all other complex animals, most of the research can be done in rodents. Dogs, cats and monkeys together make up less than .05 per cent of the total. Most of the other animals are birds (mainly chickens, including eggs more than halfway through gestation), fish and rabbits. Except in special circumstances that require the permission of the Home Secretary, all animals must be specially bred for research. Stray pets are never used. Animal studies tell researchers much more about how a medicine is likely to affect people than would be possible using non-animal methods alone. New medicines also go through extensive tests in people once the preliminary research indicates it is safe to do so.

Why don't you use alternatives?

We do. Some people may think that the researcher has a choice between an animal and a non-animal method. But the researcher has no such choice. If a validated alternative can provide the necessary information, it must be used. Whole areas of medicines research that used to have to be done in animals are now done in other ways. However, our biological knowledge is still limited, so computer simulations and test-tube methods give only part of the picture. Some questions must be addressed in the whole living body. The pharmaceutical industry is well known to work at the forefront of technology and use it to the full.

How can you justify using animals to make human medicines?

The use of animals in medicines research is a complex moral issue with no easy answer. Most of us want to do the best for people and animals but most people would accept that human health and well-being come first. As few animals as necessary should be used and they should be spared all unnecessary distress. But if we want to have new and better medicines without taking unacceptable risks with human life, then for the foreseeable future, we have to accept that animals will be needed.

Aren't medicines developed for profit?

Of course medicine manufacturers have to make profits. Today a medicine takes an average of 12 years and over £300 million to develop and there are never any guarantees, even right up to the end of that period, that the medicine will ultimately be safe and effective enough to be approved for use by patients. Only profit-making organisations can withstand this level of financial risk and fund the next generations of medicines. It is profits made today which pay for research in the future.

Some people may think that the researcher has a choice between an animal and a non-animal method. But the researcher has no such choice

---

Why are most procedures carried out without anaesthetics?

Because most procedures are too mild to justify the upset that would be caused by giving a general anaesthetic. Most procedures cause only mild or momentary distress, so it is right and proper that most experiments are conducted without anaesthesia. Giving a medicine orally, injections or taking blood would not warrant the disturbance caused by an anaesthetic in animals, any more than it would be in people.

The law requires that any pain, distress or discomfort likely to be experienced by the animal is prevented or reduced to the minimum possible given the nature of the research, for instance, by using pain killers, and by ensuring that those doing the research have all the necessary skills to perform procedures in a way that causes as little distress as possible. Any animal suffering severe pain or distress that cannot be alleviated must, by law, be humanely killed immediately, regardless of whether the object of the research has been achieved.

How quickly can animal tests be reduced?

There has already been enormous progress. Many areas of the research process that leads to a new medicine now require very few animals, one of the main reasons why there are about half as many animals used in the UK now as was the case 20 years ago.

At the same time, advances in our understanding of the genetic basis of disease mean that there is important new research being conducted that could not have been done in the past. Millions of people are affected by genetic disorders.

It is important, and morally right, to keep the use of animals to a minimum but it would be morally wrong to put our concern for animals first and thereby deny people living with incurable, and sometimes untreatable, conditions the chance of a healthier future.

Animals and people are different, so how can information from animals help?

There are enormous biological similarities between humans and other animals. Certainly, there are differences but compared to the similarities, these differences are minor. Researchers understand many of these differences and design studies to take these differences into account. As a result, most of those effects that cannot yet be predicted from computer and test-tube methods can be seen in animals.

No one expects animals to tell us everything we need to know. All new medicines are also studied in patients but only after scientists and doctors feel confident it is safe to do so. The information needed to make these judgements cannot currently be obtained from non-animal methods alone. Because of the similarities between humans and other animals, coupled with the knowledge of researchers and the veterinarians who work with them, animal studies bridge the gap between the test tube and the patient.

But what about medicines that are later found to have problems, despite animal testing?

Those same medicines have been through years of human testing as well and the problem was still not found. Yet no one says that human testing is therefore unnecessary. There are many reasons why rare side-effects may not be seen until after a medicine becomes available and a great many people are taking it (such as underlying medical conditions of which the patient and doctor were unaware or genetic factors that will only affect a small portion of the population). But it should be remembered that no one expects animal testing to give all the answers. The aim is to find out as much as realistically possible before the tests in patients begin. That way, the risks are greatly minimised and doctors have a good understanding of how tests in people should be conducted.

Isn't there a lot of repetition of animal studies when there are similar medicines to treat a medical problem?

No, that is not the case. Potential new prescription medicines that are different enough to be patentable (which means that the company is protected from copying for a limited number of years) are different enough to have varied effectiveness and safety profiles.

Data on different medicines based on the same class of molecule, for instance taxanes for breast and ovarian cancer, triptans for migraine or protease inhibitors for HIV and AIDS, are not interchangeable. Neither the company nor the Department of Health could use data from one to justify approval of another.

Nor would it be in the interest of patients to suggest that different but chemically similar medicines should not be developed. Different people respond better to different medicines within the same chemical group. In addition, people with long-term conditions are likely to need a range of medicines over the years.

New prescription medicines should not be confused with older prescription medicines on which the patent has expired and which can therefore be copied without going through the animal testing stage.

● The above information is from the Association of the British Pharmaceutical Industry's web site which can be found at www.abpi.org.uk Alternatively, see page 41 for their address details.

© ABPI – The Association of the British Pharmaceutical Industry

The benefits of animals in scientific research

Information from Huntingdon Life Sciences

There is considerable concern about the use of animals in scientific research, and all too often it is easy to lose sight of the advantages that have been generated through this work with animals.

Behind the scare stories and myths there lies an ever growing number of successes and advances in the field of human medicine. For many years, humans have benefited from the healthcare advances that animal-based research has achieved.

For example, here is a list of the average number of operations performed in the UK in a year:

- 3,000,000 operations under general anaesthetic
- 90,000 cataract operations
- 60,000 joint replacements
- 13,000 coronary bypasses
- 10,000 pacemakers implanted
- 6,000 heart valve repairs or replacements
- 4,000 heart defects corrected
- 2,500 corneal transplants
- 2,000 kidney transplants
- 400 heart/lung transplants

None of these operations or the techniques used during them would have been possible without previous animal research. It is likely that many of us will come into contact with someone who has benefited from these advances. The contribution that animals have made to human well-being is immense.

Advances continue to be made – key-hole surgery, organ transplantation, skin grafting and the latest research into the prevention of genetic diseases are all benefiting from animal research.

It is certain that any unnecessary reduction in the amount of research would have serious consequences for future research into human illness and well-being.

● The above information is from Huntingdon Life Sciences' web site which can be found at www.huntingdon.com/index.html

© Huntingdon Life Sciences

Vivisection

Information from the Young People's Trust for the Environment

Vivisection', if taken literally, means cutting apart live animals. Of course, many experiments on animals do not involve any cutting at all, but it has become the generally accepted term for any experimenting performed on animals. It is an issue which arouses strong feelings, with many organisations calling for a halt to animal testing, whilst those involved in vivisection attempt to show why it should be continued. The arguments for and against can get confusing, so before we start getting into the debate, let's look at the facts and figures.

How many experiments are carried out?

In the United Kingdom, just under three million experiments are carried out on animals each year. According to government figures, 2,716,587 'procedures' (a politically-correct term for 'experiments') were performed in 1996. Over the last 18 years, the annual number of experiments has decreased by two and a half million.

What are the experiments for?

The animal experiments were carried out for the following reasons:

- Developing treatments for new diseases 43%
- Biological and medical research 32%
- Safety testing (less than 0.2% on cosmetics) 8%
- Animals bred with an inherited genetic defect for medical research 14%
- Developing new methods of diagnosis 2%

Which animals are used in research?

Using figures provided by the Home Office (1996), it is possible to be fairly precise as to how many procedures were performed on each type of animal:

Rats, mice and other rodents (bred for research) – 85% (2,309,099 experiments)

Fish, birds, amphibians and reptiles – 10% (271,659 experiments)

Small mammals other than rodents mainly rabbits and ferrets – 2.2% (59,765 experiments)

Sheep, cows, pigs and other large mammals – 2.2% (59,765 experiments)

Dogs and cats (bred for research) – 0.4% (10,866 experiments)

Monkeys such as marmosets and macaques – 0.2% (5,433 experiments)

Presumably in most cases, animals which have been used for one experiment cannot be used for any others because of the polluting effects of the substances they are testing. It is likely that these animals will be 'disposed' of.

Who funds the experiments?

According to 'Uncaged', an anti-vivisection group, 52% of these experiments are funded by commercial concerns. A further 29% of funding comes from universities, but universities get most of their research funding from commercial concerns. Therefore most of the money for research comes from commercial sources – mainly in the medical and industrial sectors. The pharmaceutical industry is now the largest in the world. Popular drugs can be huge money earners, with big-sellers like aspirin earning over one million dollars per day in sales. 20,000 tonnes of aspirin are consumed each year in the USA alone. This is equivalent to 225 tablets per inhabitant.

Who checks that the experiments are necessary and carried out properly?

Testing on laboratory animals is regulated in the UK by the Animals (Scientific Procedures) Act 1986. The Animals Procedures Committee was set up by the Act and is in charge of deciding whether experiments should take place or not. However, the Committee of 21 inspectors has to supervise 2.71 million experiments carried out by 5,600 vivisectors throughout the country, so in reality, it would be fairly easy to abuse the system, if an experimenter felt it was in his/her best interests to do so.

What do experiments on animals prove?

Many animal experiments are performed to highlight any potentially harmful effects of newly-developed medicines and chemical substances on humans. In some cases, researchers try to mimic conditions affecting humans (e.g. cancer, cystic fibrosis, arthritis, etc.) in the animals they are experimenting on, to see if new medicines will be effective in treating them. The Research Defence Society (a pro-vivisection organisation) claims that inherited diseases such as cystic fibrosis are now being accurately reproduced in specially bred genetically altered laboratory mice.

The above are the facts. They say what is actually happening in this country (and in America). What follows can be seen as the arguments put forward by people with completely opposing views. The anti-vivisectionists claim that vivisection is outdated, unnecessary, cruel, and produces misleading results. Pro-vivisectionists say that animal experiments are vital to the advancement of medicine, that care is taken to limit the suffering inflicted on animals and that vivisection is the only accurate way to test responses of entire living organisms to chemicals, rather than those of an isolated section of body tissue.

• The above information is an extract from a factsheet produced by the Young People's Trust for the Environment. Factsheets are available on their web site at www.yptenc.org.uk Alternatively, see page 41 for their address details.

Frequently asked questions

Information from FRAME

Animal research

Why is animal research carried out?
Animals are used

- to improve our knowledge of how biological systems function,
- to study the causes and effects of diseases in humans and other animals, so that we can develop new methods for diagnosis and treatment, and
- for education and training, for example in medical and veterinary colleges.

In addition, the laws of all major countries require some animal testing of medical and veterinary products and some other chemicals, for example pesticides, to identify any potential hazard to humans, animals and the environment.

To what extent do research animals experience pain, suffering or distress?
Researchers in the UK are legally required to minimise any pain, suffering or distress experienced by laboratory animals. This can be achieved, for example, by the use of anaesthetics and pain-killing drugs. Nevertheless, animals can still suffer to some extent. Merely housing an animal within a laboratory can cause some suffering due to loss of freedom and restrictions on normal behaviour. The extent of such suffering is likely to vary from species to species.

Where can I find information on the number of animals used for scientific research?
Each year, the Home Office publishes detailed statistics on the number of procedures conducted on living animals. A review of the statistics is published by FRAME each year in *FRAME NEWS* and *ATLA*.

The alternatives

How effective are the various alternative techniques?
The alternative methods that have been developed have been effective in reducing the number of animals used in many areas of scientific research. For example, 3-dimensional models of human skin are now used extensively by cosmetic companies to test their products. Computer modelling and cell-culture systems are used by the pharmaceutical industry to screen potential new drugs for activity and potential toxicity, before any animal studies are conducted. These enable many thousands of chemicals to be tested in one experiment, and it means that many fewer animals are used.

Is total replacement of animal research possible in the future?
This will depend on many factors: the level of funding applied to developing replacement alternatives; our increased understanding of human and animal biology; and whether replacement alternatives are

accepted by regulatory bodies. At present, total replacement of laboratory animals is a long way off but we are making progress with developing alternatives for specific toxicity tests and for use in education.

Legal issues

Does the law adequately protect animal welfare?
The Animals (Scientific Procedures) Act 1986 requires that the Three Rs (reduction, refinement and replacement) should be applied wherever possible, to minimise animal suffering and to reduce the number of animals used. This Act also requires the Home Secretary, in consultation with a team of experts, to weigh up the balance between the costs to the animals and the potential benefits of a research proposal, before allowing any experiment to go ahead. However, there is scope for improving the implementation and effectiveness of this legislation. For example, the cost-benefit assessment should be made more rigorous and open.

What does FRAME want from the Government?
We want more effective application of current legislation. In some areas of research we also want more regulations, for example in transgenic research where the current controls are insufficient to cope with the welfare problems arising from this new technology. We also want the UK Government to exert more pressure on the governments of other countries to encourage the use of valid alternative methods, such as the in-vitro techniques for the production of monoclonal antibodies.

- The above information is from FRAME's web site which can be found at www.frame.org.uk Alternatively, see page 41 for their address details.

© *FRAME (Fund for the Replacement of Animals in Medical Experiments)*

The use of animals in scientific procedures

Information from the Home Office

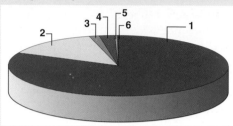

Types of animals used in medical research

Numbers relate to regulated procedures on animals in Great Britain in 2000.

1. 82%. Rats, mice and other rodents. All specially bred laboratory species.
2. 14%. Fish, amphibians, reptiles and birds (including many fertilised hen's eggs).
3. 1.5% Small mammals other than rodents, mostly rabbits and ferrets.
4. 2.3%. Sheep, cows, pigs and other large mammals.
5. 0.4%. Dogs and cats. Specially bred for research. No strays or unwanted pets can be used.
6. 0.1%. Monkeys, such as mormosets and macaques. Chimpanzees, orang-utans and gorillas have not been used in this country for over 20 years and their use is now banned.

The Animals (Scientific Procedures) Act 1986 protects all living vertebrate animals (plus one species of octopus) used in scientific procedures in Great Britain. Other invertebrates, animals such as fruit flies and worms, are also used in research, but are not protected under British law.

Source: Research Defence Society (RDS)

The Government is very conscious of public concerns about the use of animals in experiments and other scientific procedures and accepts that many people would like to stop all such work. Unfortunately, this cannot yet be done without halting important areas of medical and scientific research. The development of many new drugs, and medical and veterinary technologies, which reduce suffering and prevent large-scale infections, have depended on and continue to depend on the use of animals. Procedures involving animals form an essential part of medical and pharmaceutical research and produce vital information and real therapeutic benefits.

This use of animals is regulated by the Animals (Scientific Procedures) Act 1986, which is widely viewed as the most rigorous piece of legislation of its type in the world. It puts into effect, and in some ways exceeds, European Union Directive 86/609/EEC and offers a high level of protection to animals whilst recognising the need to use animals in medical research, the development of new medicines and scientific testing. It also has sufficient flexibility to allow the latest ideas and technology to be taken into account when deciding whether the use of animals is justified.

Under the Act, both personal and project licences are required. These ensure that those doing the work are qualified and suitable; that alternatives to animals are used wherever possible; that the number of animals used is minimised; and that any suffering or other harmful effects experienced by the animals have been weighed against the potential benefits (to humans or animals). Special conditions, tailored to each project, control and minimise any pain or suffering. In addition, work can only be carried out at establishments which meet high standards and which have suitable veterinary and animal welfare personnel.

Animals (Scientific Procedures) Inspectorate

Home Office Inspectors assess applications for licences and certificates and advise the Home Secretary on whether, and on what terms, they should be granted. When assessing research proposals, the Inspectorate ensures that full consideration is given to alternatives, not only the replacement of procedures with others which do not use animals, but also the reduction of the number of animals used and the refinement of procedures to minimise pain and suffering. These are known as the three Rs. Inspectors visit establishments, mainly without notice, to ensure that the terms and conditions of licences and certificates are being met.

The Inspectors are all highly qualified and experienced in medicine or veterinary science. They have very high professional standards directed to ensuring that animals are protected within the terms of the Act and the conditions of the licences.

Animal Procedures Committee

The Animal Procedures Committee (APC) is an independent body set up under the Act to advise the Home Secretary on matters concerned with the Act and his functions under it. Excluding the Chairman, there must be a minimum of 12 members, one must be a lawyer and at least two-thirds must be medical practitioners, veterinary surgeons or have qualifications or experience in a biological subject. At least half of the members must not have held a licence to carry out procedures on animals within the last six years and animal welfare interests must be adequately represented. All appointments to the Animal Procedures Committee are announced publicly.

When there is doubt about whether to license a particular piece of work, the Home Secretary may seek advice from the Animal Procedures Committee or other independent assessors. The Home Secretary may refer other matters to the Committee and the APC may also consider topics of its own choosing. The Committee must consider both the legitimate requirements of science and industry and the protection of animals against avoidable suffering and unnecessary use. Each year, the Committee makes a report on its activities to the Home Secretary. This is published through the Stationery Office.

Annual statistics

Each year, the Home Office publishes detailed statistics on the use of animals in scientific procedures in Great Britain. In 1998, 2.66 million procedures were carried out – a reduction of more than 25% since the introduction of the Act and, with the exception of 1997, the lowest total for over 40 years. There have been occasional small annual rises, but the overall trend over the past 20 years has been downwards. This has been largely due to the efforts of researchers, with the encouragement of the Inspectorate, in seeking alternatives to animals and in improving research methods to reduce the number of animals used.

Where do the animals come from?

Stray pets are never used in scientific procedures. For reliable results, most experiments depend on animals being free of infection or disease, which can best be achieved if they come from a known source with fully documented breeding histories. In addition, cats and dogs must be obtained from designated (licensed) breeding establishments and all mice, rats, hamsters, guinea pigs, rabbits, quail, primates, ferrets and gerbils must be obtained from designated breeders or suppliers. Exemptions from this rule are rarely granted. Mice and rats account for the vast majority (over 80%) of the animals used. Dogs and cats can only be used if no other species is suitable and account for only 0.3% of all procedures (three in every thousand).

Monkeys and other primates

No project licence authorising the use of monkeys or other primates in scientific procedures may be granted unless the Home Secretary is satisfied that no other species is suitable or that animals of another suitable species cannot be obtained. No chimpanzees or other great apes have ever been used under the 1986 Act and Ministers announced on 6 November 1997 that the use of great apes would not be allowed. The Home Secretary has also announced a ban on the use of wild-caught primates unless an exceptional case can be established. Primates are used in less than 0.2% of all scientific procedures (less than two in every thousand) and in 1998, only 4 wild-caught primates were used.

Validity of animal procedures

Some people suggest that information derived from procedures on animals cannot be extended to humans or other species. These views do not reflect the consensus in the wider scientific community. There are physiological or bio-chemical differences between species, but there are greater similarities. Species differences are taken into account within the design of the project and the results of testing a new drug, for example, on animals can be used to predict the effect on humans.

Animal experiments form only a small fraction of biomedical research and testing – most is done using computers, test tubes, cell cultures, lower forms of life etc. But in many areas there is still no alternative to using living animals.

Regulatory toxicity testing

National and international regulatory bodies require that products as varied as industrial cleaners and cosmetics are safe for humans, other animals and the environment. Unfortunately, until reliable alternatives have been developed, this means in practice that tests have to be carried out on animals. This country has taken a leading role in Europe in encouraging the application of the three Rs whilst ensuring that the tests remain acceptable to the regulatory authorities. The UK was prominent, for example, in encouraging an international collaborative study to reduce the need for the much-criticised LD50 toxicity test.

• The above information is from the Home Office's web site which can be found at www.homeoffice.gov.uk

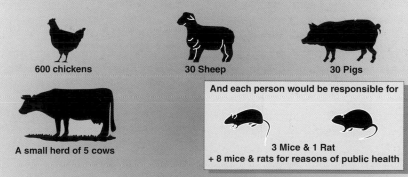

The use of animals by you . . .

. . . if you are an average UK citizen

The numbers in the illustration below show the use of animals as food, the number of animals destroyed as pests and the number of animals used in medical research per person in the UK during their lifetime based on a life span of 70 years.

600 chickens

30 Sheep

30 Pigs

A small herd of 5 cows

And each person would be responsible for

3 Mice & 1 Rat + 8 mice & rats for reasons of public health

The 600 chickens, 5 cows, 30 sheep and 30 pigs represent the number of animals the average UK citizen will eat in their lifetime.

We can see that during our lifetime researchers will use approximately 3 mice and 1 rat on our behalf to develop new medicines, vaccines etc. The use of monkeys, cats and dogs per human lifetime is so small that it amounts to only a tiny fraction of a single animal.

We can contrast this with the fact that during our 70-year life pest control agencies will kill, usually by poisoning, 8 rats and mice on behalf of each of us.

Source: Biomedical Research Education Trust

Alternatives

Alternatives to animal experiments in medical research. Information from the Dr Hadwen Trust

Opinion polls show that the public are largely opposed in principle to animal experiments. Many of us make a conscious choice to purchase toiletries and household products that have not been tested on animals. Yet when it comes to medicines, we are not given this choice. At present, much conventional medical research relies on animal experiments and all new medicines are tested on animals. Even complementary therapies, such as herbalism, homoeopathy, and acupuncture are being investigated by some scientists in animals.

So what can be done to end the use of animals by medical science? One practical solution is to develop alternative research methods that can replace animals – methods that are not only more humane, but more reliable and accurate than animal experiments.

These humane alternatives include a variety of techniques, such as cell and tissue cultures, computer modelling, molecular or test-tube methods, and micro-organisms. Studying humans is ultimately the most relevant form of medical research of all, and finding new, safe and ethical ways to study patients and healthy volunteers can also provide alternatives to invasive animal experiments.

Can alternatives really replace animal experiments? Yes, they can and they have already had a big impact worldwide. Since the 1970s animal experiments have roughly halved, a reduction that has been largely attributed to replacement by alternative techniques. Official estimates for animal experiments globally are more than 100 million a year, so this means that tens of millions of animals have been spared from the laboratory thanks to alternatives.

There have been some impressive examples of alternatives replacing routine animal tests.

By Carol Newman, Scientific Officer, Dr Hadwen Trust

Insulin, used to treat diabetics, was once tested for purity and strength in mice. Each batch of insulin was checked by a test using 600 mice. Now chemical analysis does the job more accurately and at less cost.

Pregnancy testing once involved injecting urine samples into rabbits, who were then killed and their ovaries removed. Now pregnancy testing is a simple test-tube procedure.

Diagnosis of tuberculosis once required injecting infected samples into guinea pigs, but it can now be done using tissue culture tests, saving the lives of thousands of animals.

These are just a few examples of how alternatives have replaced animal tests. With continued effort and the development of increasingly sophisticated technology even more can be achieved in the future. Despite their enormous potential, very few organisations exist to encourage and fund alternatives to animal experiments. One of the leading charities working in this area is the Dr Hadwen Trust. From small beginnings thirty years ago the Trust has grown to be one of the country's foremost experts on alternatives to vivisection.

The Trust is founded on anti-

vivisection principles and is opposed to all animal experiments. Its mission is to promote alternatives and to find new non-animal research methods that can actually replace procedures that currently use animals. Over the years the Trust has supported many different types of alternatives for research into an enormous variety of human illnesses.

For example, the Dr Hadwen Trust funded a computer model of human teeth and jawbone, for use in dental research. Dental devices and surgery for serious deformities such as cleft lip and palate, are often tested on animals, including dogs, cats and pigs. The computer model is based on data from human volunteers and exploits engineering technology originally designed for testing buildings and bridges. It was the first model to predict responses of human teeth to dental treatments, and it is now being used by other scientists in Japan and Germany, some of whom had been doing animal experiments.

Computer programs that model various body systems, and on which simulated investigations can be conducted, are providing exciting new alternatives to experiments on animals. Computer models of the heart, brain and immune system are helping scientists to unravel the complexities of the human body, its response to illness, and the effects of drugs. Virtual reality, 3-D computer simulations through which a user can 'move' and interact by wearing special glasses and gloves, is taking us into the realms of yesterday's science fiction. One of the most complex computer models ever attempted, a virtual human, is now under development in America, for use in simulated experiments.

Another of the Trust's computer projects is Fetal Charlotte, a model of the human placenta and foetus, for studying problems affecting unborn babies. Simulated experiments can be conducted on the computer model, as an alternative to research on pregnant animals, notably rabbits, sheep, and mice. Fetal Charlotte quickly proved its usefulness by explaining changes in blood-flow seen in women developing potentially dangerous complications in pregnancy. Now further versions of Fetal Charlotte have been developed to investigate heart defects and placental malfunctions.

Interactive computer models are available for use in teaching physiology, pharmacology and anatomy in place of dissections or experiments on anaesthetised animals. In drug development, computer programs based on existing knowledge of the shape, structure and activity of molecules, combined with data on the human body, are being used to help design improved drugs and screen them for safety. The rapid advances being made in this field of technology make the future potential of computers to replace animals enormous.

The ability to grow cells and tissues in flasks in the laboratory is also helping to replace experiments on animals. Cell cultures are now used in many medical fields and have contributed enormously to our understanding of cancer, Parkinson's disease, and AIDS. They are routinely used in vaccine production, safety testing, drug development and to diagnose disease.

Cells and tissues can be obtained from humans after death (postmortem), as biopsies (small samples of tissue usually taken for diagnosis), as waste from surgery, or placentas. It is important that human cells, rather than animal cells, are used for medical research, to avoid the problem of relating results from one species to another. To encourage the use of human cells and tissues the Dr Hadwen Trust helped to establish the first national UK Human Tissue Bank at Leicester. The tissue bank collects, stores and distributes human tissues for research.

Some research that once used animals is now being done with human cell cultures. One example, the US National Cancer Institute now uses screens of human tumour cells to identify potential new anti-cancer drugs, instead of tests on

leukaemic mice. As a result, the Institute's use of animals has dropped by more than 5 million a year.

The Dr Hadwen Trust has pioneered cell culture as alternatives to animal experiments in diabetes, rheumatism, AIDS, cancer, brain research, and more. In a recent project, Trust researchers cultured human lens cells that thrive in the laboratory and can be used to replace animals in cataracts research. Cataracts affect the lens of the eye and, if left untreated, can lead to blindness. A shortage of donated human eyes for research means that animals, such as chicks, rabbits, frogs and monkeys, are used instead. The Trust's researchers have developed more than 50 different human lens cell cultures, and distributed them around the world, for use in place of animals in the study of cataracts and eye development.

One of the best methods of medical research is to study the whole human being. New scanning and imaging techniques are making it increasingly possible to 'look inside' the human body without surgery, enabling ethical studies of patients and healthy volunteers.

By changing the face of science, the Dr Hadwen Trust is creating a brighter future for both humans and animals. Who knows what further achievements will be made with alternatives in the 21st century?

At one time the human brain was exceedingly difficult to study and it could only be closely examined after death, or during brain surgery. To study the living, functioning brain, scientists would implant electrodes into the brains of animals and make recordings from them. Thanks to modern physics, a range of brain imaging techniques, such as EEG, PET, and MRI, are revolutionising brain research by enabling

scientists to non-invasively study the intact functioning human brain.

One of the latest scanning machines is called MEG. MEG detects magnetic fields to create magnetic maps of the brain. It is highly sensitive and can detect tiny areas of brain activity very accurately. The Dr Hadwen Trust helped to fund the only MEG facility in the country to study human vision and epileptic patients, as an alternative to severe and invasive experiments on cats and monkeys.

Another innovative technique, TMS, uses a strong magnetic pulse, to temporarily disrupt the brain. This method has been used by Trust researchers in experiments to harmlessly mimic 'brain damage' with human volunteers, instead of inflicting permanent brain damage on monkeys.

By changing the face of science, the Dr Hadwen Trust is creating a brighter future for both humans and animals. Who knows what further achievements will be made with alternatives in the 21st century? One thing is certain, however: the impetus to develop alternatives has always come from the animal protection movement. Thirty years ago many scientists protested they had already done everything they could to replace animals and dismissed further progress with alternatives. Since then great strides have been made and many animals have been saved by new alternative techniques. To maintain this progress, the scientific community must continue to be urged to actively pursue humane research techniques to replace animal experiments.

• For a free information pack about the work of the Trust telephone 01462 436819 or write to the Dr Hadwen Trust, 84A Tilehouse Street, Hitchin, Herts, SG5 2DY. Alternatively visit the Trust's website at www.drhadwentrust.org.uk

• The above article is about alternatives to animal experiments and the work of the Dr Hadwen Trust. It was written for an online animal rights magazine called Ooze and can be seen there presently at www.oozemagazine.co.uk

Hunting – focus on the figures

Information from the Countryside Alliance

There are 318 registered hound packs in England and Wales:

– 184 Foxhound packs recognised by the Masters of Foxhounds' Association

– 20 Harrier packs recognised by the Association of Masters of Harriers and Beagles

– 3 Deer packs recognised by the Masters of Deer Hounds' Association

– 72 Beagle packs recognised by the Association of Masters of Harriers and Beagles

– 10 Basset packs recognised by the Masters of Basset Hounds' Association

– 20 Mink packs recognised by the Masters of Mink Hounds' Association

– 9 Fell packs recognised by the Central Committee of Fell Packs

- 50% were founded before 1869 and 29% post 1930.
- Only 36 hunts are the result of amalgamation: 33% pre 1969, 33% 1970-1984 and 33% post 1985.
- 272 packs have total registered hunting country amounting to 133,600 square miles. 26% of this is not hunted for reasons of safety (motorways, roads, railways and development), only 3% is not hunted because permission is denied.

- The majority of hunts own their property, facilities and equipment. Their inventory includes 200 owned kennels, 152 slaughter houses, 145 incinerators, 309 houses, 64 flats, 6460 acres of covert and 1440 acres of paddocks.
- They own 241 lorries, 188 trucks and pick ups and 23 quad bikes and ATVs.
- They own 834 horses probably worth some £1.7million, 15,000 'entered' hounds and 4178 'unentered' hounds.
- There are 748 joint or single hunt Masters (average 2.7 per hunt). They have 510 full-time hunt employees (average 2.6 per hunt) and 325 part-time employees (average 1.7 per hunt). Total employees plus 'professional' masters amount to about 950.
- 260 hunts have the services of 3115 'puppy walkers', an average of 12 per hunt.
- 273 hunts have a total of 28,300 subscribers, including members (100 per hunt).
- 205 hunts have a total of 39,000 supporters' club members (190 per hunt).
- 158 mounted packs average 13 mounted visitors per hunting day. This is an annual attendance of 176,700 day visitors per season.
- 273 hunts hold a total of 18,000 hunting days each season.
- Total annual 'attendance' at all meets is 1,280,000 persons of which 541,000 (42%) are on horses and 741,000 (58%) are on foot.
- Fox hunts caught 13,987 foxes last season, of which 8,896 (64%) were 'above ground' and 5,091 (36%) were dug.
- 285 hunts organise over 21 different types of equestrian and social events. Each year this totals 3,950 functions with an overall attendance of 1,326,000 people which raise £4.5million.
- Total hunt income is £14.9 million per annum. This derives 57% from member and subscriber charges, 30% from hunt fundraising and 13% from other sources.
- Hunt revenue expenditure is £14.07 million per annum. 40% of expenditure is direct employment. Annual capital expenditure averages £2.9million in total.
- Fallen stock: 200 hunts collect

366,000 head of fallen stock per annum. This is an average of 1,830 head per hunt. 80% of hunts estimate that demand for this service from farmers is growing by up to 50% per annum.

- These 200 hunts spend a total of £3.37 million annually on collecting this stock. This is an average of £18,000 per hunt and £9.20 per animal collected.

Hunt supporters

- 124 supporters' clubs associated with foxhounds, staghounds, beagles and harriers and terriers and lurchers. Total membership is 21,576.
- 45% of all members are female, 13% are under 18 and 34% are a part of a family group.
- Members have a diverse range of occupations, most frequent are:
  – Retired 20%
  – Agricultural workers 17%
  – 'Professionals' 14%
- Membership is two-thirds 'rural' based:
  – living in rural situations 41%
  – living in a village 23%
  – living in a town 17%
  – living in a city 7%
- Ethnic grouping: 80% of clubs have only 'white' members. Seven clubs have an average of 2-3 members who are 'non-white', nine clubs have just 1-2 'non-white' members.
- 81% of clubs follow only their own hunt. Half of the clubs have some link with at least one other club.
- It is estimated that the average supporters' club member will attend more than 20 'hunting' events within a season.
- 89 clubs state that in addition to their average membership of 170 people, a further 87 non-members (average) are regular visitors to the hunts they support. Over the 124 packs, this is a further 10,700 non-member followers.
- 7.5% of hunt supporters follow the hunt by car.
- 15% follow the hunt on foot.
- 6% follow the hunt on motor bikes.
- 4% follow the hunt on bicycles.
- These 124 supporters' clubs organise 1,680 social or fund-raising functions each year, an average of 14 for each club.

- 260 charities (50 different ones) are supported by 123 of these 124 clubs. Over 2 per club.
- Annual membership costs between £6 and £12 with some flexibility.
- Were there to be a ban on hunting with dogs, 260 club members (1.2%) might follow blood hounds, 466 members (2.2%) might follow drag hounds.

• The above information is from the Countryside Alliance's web site which can be found at www.countryside-alliance.org Alternatively, see page 41 for their address details.

© *Countryside Alliance*

The Countryside Alliance's policy on welfare

Animal rights vs. animal welfare

Proper care and protection of animals is a matter of welfare – not rights. The animal rights philosophy gives rise to countless absurdities and paradoxes. The concept of rights is inoperable without the linked concept of responsibilities which cannot practicably be applied to animals. The advancement of animal welfare ensures a sustainable relationship between mankind, the production of animal products and wildlife management. The Alliance recommends:

- A Royal Commission should be established to examine the use and management of animals by mankind.

Animal welfare legislation

UK animal welfare legislation is piecemeal and incoherent; it requires a thorough overhaul and consolidation. The Alliance recommends:

- The prohibition of the intentional infliction of unnecessary suffering on any mammal by any means, as the basic tenet of animal welfare legislation.
- Ensuring the continuation of properly managed country sports to concord with this principle.

Animal husbandry

The Countryside Alliance endorses the Five Freedoms established to define good animal welfare by the Government-appointed Farm Animal Welfare Council. This will inevitably increase costs of production, but imposition in the UK, without taking steps to prevent the import of food produced more cheaply abroad, will simply put the British producers out of business. The Alliance recommends:

- International enforcement of reasonable animal welfare standards should be incorporated into global trade negotiations.
- Food product labelling should be developed so as to give consumers the option to make informed choices in selecting their goods.

Live exports and animal transportation

The live export of farm animals over long distances is an important concern. Yet the transport of animals need not result in poor welfare. Over-zealous implementation of EU directives is forcing the closure of small abattoirs. This results in longer journey times to slaughter, with adverse welfare implications. The Alliance recommends:

- Immediate action is needed to safeguard remaining rural abattoirs in order to facilitate slaughter close to the farm.
- Transport distances, vehicle facilities, rest times and supervision which equate with acceptable welfare standards have been defined in law and must now be rigorously enforced.
- European measures to make long journey times to slaughter unnecessary.

© *Countryside Alliance*

Hunting with dogs

Summary and conclusions of the Committee of Inquiry into Hunting with Dogs in England and Wales

Hunting

Hunting with dogs is a diverse activity.

There are about 200 registered packs of hounds (mainly foxhounds but also some harriers) in England and Wales which hunt foxes, plus a number of unregistered packs in Wales. Most packs have mounted followers but a number, including the Fell packs in Cumbria and the footpacks in Wales, are followed on foot only. The Welsh gunpacks use dogs to flush foxes to waiting guns.

The registered packs are estimated to kill some 21,000-25,000 foxes a year. About 40% of the foxes killed by the registered packs are killed in the autumn/cub hunting season. In Wales and other upland areas, a high proportion of foxes are dug out, using terriers, and shot. Outside the registered packs, many more foxes are dug out and shot or are killed by people using lurchers or other 'long dogs'. Some of these activities are carried out by farmers, landowners and gamekeepers. Others involve trespass.

There are three registered staghound packs in the Devon and Somerset area. They kill about 160 red deer a year in total, excluding injured deer which they dispatch. This probably represents about 15% of the numbers which need to be culled in the area to maintain a stable population.

There are about a hundred registered packs of hounds (beagles, bassets and harriers) which hunt hares. They kill about 1,650 hares a season, a very small percentage of the number killed by shooting.

There are some 24 registered hare coursing clubs, which kill about 250 hares a year in total, and a small number of other unregistered clubs. But there is a good deal of illegal hunting/coursing in some areas.

The 20 minkhound packs kill somewhere between 400-1,400 mink a season. The number is thought to be considerably smaller than that killed by trapping and shooting.

Animal welfare

The issues of cruelty and animal welfare are central to the debate about hunting. Animal welfare is essentially concerned with assessing the ability of an animal to cope with its environment: if an animal is having difficulty in coping with its environment, or is failing to cope, then its welfare may be regarded as poor. This judgment is distinct from any ethical or moral judgments about the way in which the animal is being treated.

Except in relation to deer, little scientific work has been done to assess the impact of hunting on the welfare of the four quarry species. Because it is not possible to ask an animal about its welfare, or to know what is going on inside its head, it is necessary to draw up some indicators which enable one to make a judgment. The precise nature of these indicators will vary depending on the animal concerned but they will usually comprise a mixture of physiological indicators and behavioural indicators. But, because they are only indicators, there is often room for argument about the extent to which a particular finding indicates poor welfare as opposed to, for example, exertion that can be regarded as falling within natural limits. It is also necessary to consider whether the assessment of welfare should be on an absolute or comparative basis.

The issues of cruelty and animal welfare are central to the debate about hunting

---

Animal welfare is concerned with the welfare of the individual animal, not the management of the wider population. In assessing the impact of hunting on animal welfare we are persuaded that it is necessary to look at it on a relative, rather than an absolute, basis. It should not be compared with only the best, or the worst, of the alternatives. Nor is it right to justify hunting by reference to the welfare implications of illegal methods of control.

In the event of a ban on hunting, it seems probable that farmers and others would resort more frequently to other methods to kill foxes, deer, hares and perhaps mink. There would be a mixture of motives: pest control; the value of the carcass; and the recreational value to be derived from shooting. It follows that the welfare of animals which are hunted should be compared with the welfare which, on a realistic assessment, would be likely to result from the legal methods used by farmers and others to manage the population of these animals in the event of a ban on hunting.

Deer

The hunting of a red deer typically comprises a series of intermittent flights in which the deer exerts itself maximally in order to escape from the hounds. An average hunt which ends in the killing of the deer lasts about 3 hours. Scientific studies show that, at the end of a chase, deer have very low levels of carbohydrate (glycogen) in their muscles and that this largely explains why they are forced to stop.

There is a lack of firm information about the wounding rates which arise from stalking/shooting deer. Comparing the welfare implications of hunting and stalking/shooting deer is a complex matter, requiring the balancing of the welfare of all the deer that are hunted against the welfare of the numbers of shot deer which are wounded.

Although there are still substantial areas of disagreement, there is now a better understanding of the physiological changes which occur when a deer is hunted. Most scientists agree that deer are likely to suffer in the final stages of hunting. The available evidence does not enable us to resolve the disagreement about the point at which, during the hunt, the welfare of the deer becomes seriously compromised. There is also a lack of firm information about what happens to deer which escape, although the available research suggests that they are likely to recover.

Stalking, if carried out to a high standard and with the availability of a dog or dogs to help find any wounded deer that escape, is in principle the better method of culling deer from an animal welfare perspective. In particular, it obviates the need to chase the deer in the way which occurs in hunting.

A great deal depends, however, on the skill and care taken by the stalker. It is unfortunate that there is no reliable information on wounding rates, even in Scotland where stalking is carried out extensively. In the event of a ban on hunting, there is a risk that a greater number of deer than at present would be shot by less skilful shooters, in which case wounding rates would increase. Consideration should be given to requiring all stalkers to prove their competence by demonstrating that they had undertaken appropriate training.

Foxes

The three main aspects of fox-hunting which give rise to concern on welfare grounds are: the chase; the 'kill' by the hounds above ground; and digging-out/terrierwork.

There is a lack of scientific evidence about the welfare implications of hunting, although some post-mortem reports have been received. The welfare implications of hunting need to be compared with those which arise from other methods such as shooting, and snaring.

The evidence which we have seen suggests that, in the case of the killing of a fox by hounds above ground, death is not always effected

by a single bite to the neck or shoulders by the leading hound resulting in the dislocation of the cervical vertebrae. In a proportion of cases it results from massive injuries to the chest and vital organs, although insensibility and death will normally follow within a matter of seconds once the fox is caught. There is a lack of firm scientific evidence about the effect on the welfare of a fox of being closely pursued, caught and killed above ground by hounds. We are satisfied, nevertheless, that this experience seriously compromises the welfare of the fox.

Although there is no firm scientific evidence, we are satisfied that the activity of digging-out and shooting a fox involves a serious compromise of its welfare, bearing in mind the often protracted nature of the process and the fact that the fox is prevented from escaping.

It is likely that, in the event of a ban on hunting, many farmers and landowners would resort to a greater degree than at present to other methods to control the numbers of foxes. We cannot say if this would lead to more, or fewer, foxes being killed than at present.

None of the legal methods of fox control is without difficulty from an animal welfare perspective. Both snaring and shooting can have serious adverse welfare implications.

Our tentative conclusion is that lamping using rifles, if carried out properly and in appropriate circumstances, has fewer adverse welfare implications than hunting, including digging-out. However, in areas where lamping is not feasible

or safe, there would be a greater use of other methods. We are less confident that the use of shotguns, particularly in daylight, is preferable to hunting from a welfare perspective. We consider that the use of snaring is a particular cause for concern.

In practice, it is likely that some mixture of all of these methods would be used. In the event of a ban on hunting, it is possible that the welfare of foxes in upland areas could be affected adversely, unless dogs could be used, at least to flush foxes from cover.

Hares

There are two areas of welfare concern in respect of hare hunting and coursing: the chase and the 'kill'. Although no scientific studies have been carried out, there is evidence that, in the case of coursing, there can be a significant delay before a hare which has been caught by the dogs is dispatched.

There is a lack of firm scientific evidence about the effect on the welfare of a hare of being closely pursued, caught and killed by hounds during hunting. We are satisfied, nevertheless, that although death and insensibility will normally follow within a matter of seconds, this experience seriously compromises the welfare of the hare.

We are similarly satisfied that being pursued, caught and killed by dogs during coursing seriously compromises the welfare of the hare. It is clear, moreover, that, if the dog or dogs catch the hare, they do not always kill it quickly. There can also sometimes be a significant delay, in 'driven' coursing, before the 'picker up' reaches the hare and dispatches it (if it is not already dead). In the case of 'walked up' coursing, the delay is likely to be even longer.

In the event of a ban on hunting and coursing hares, it seems likely that a few more would be shot than at present. There are concerns about the welfare implications of shooting hares because of wounding rates.

Mink

There have been no scientific studies of the welfare implications of hunting in relation to mink.

There is a lack of firm scientific evidence about the welfare implications of hunting mink. There seems reason to suppose, however, that being closely pursued, caught and killed by hounds, or being dug out or bolted, seriously compromises the welfare of the mink. The kill, by the hounds or by shooting, is normally quick once the mink is caught. In the absence of hunting, more mink would probably be killed by shooting and, mainly, trapping. These methods involve welfare implications but we do not have sufficient evidence to conclude how they compare with those raised by hunting.

The welfare of other animals incidentally affected by hunting

Concerns have been expressed about the welfare of wildlife incidentally affected by hunting and of farm animals and pets.

There is some evidence that hunting incidentally affects the welfare of wildlife. In particular, we have been informed about the stopping-up of badger setts and a few isolated cases of disturbance to otter – both of which are protected species – and wildfowl during mink hunting. The frequency of such incidents is disputed.

The welfare of pets which are attacked by hounds is clearly compromised, and their owners often suffer great distress.

The welfare of the hounds and horses

Concerns have been expressed about the welfare of hounds and the horses involved in hunting. These have tended to focus on injuries or deaths of hounds on roads or railway lines; injuries to terriers during terrierwork; and the common practice of putting hounds down at the end of their working lives. In relation to horses, concerns are sometimes expressed about the injuries received during hunting.

We have received evidence of injuries to terriers during terrierwork. This clearly involves some compromise of the terrier's welfare when it occurs.

We have received no evidence that hunting, in general, raises greater concerns about the welfare of the horses and dogs involved than other activities such as horse racing or greyhound racing, except for small number of deaths or injuries to hounds which result from straying on roads or railways lines. There are other concerns about the hunts' practice in putting down hounds which are considered too old to hunt and about the numbers of hounds which might be put down in the event of a ban. Similarly, there are concerns over the fate of surplus horses if hunting were to be banned, and of retired racehorses. Strictly speaking, these matters do not raise animal welfare concerns provided that the hounds and horses are destroyed humanely. Rather, they raise ethical issues, which are outside our terms of reference. But any need to put down hounds or horses, in the event of a ban, could be minimised if there was a suitable lead-in time before it was implemented.

• The above information is an extract from the summary of *The Final Report of the Committee of Inquiry into Hunting with Dogs in England and Wales*, details of which can be found at the Hunting Enquiry web site at www.huntinginquiry.gov.uk

Scotland bans fox-hunting

Threat of 'rivers of blood' if rest of UK follows suit

By Kirsty Scott

Downing Street was warned last night that there will be 'rivers of blood' across the British countryside if Westminster follows the lead of the Scottish parliament, which last night banned fox-hunting in a historic and symbolic move.

After more than six hours of debate, MSPs passed the Protection of Wild Mammals (Scotland) bill by 83 to 36, with five abstentions. Even its supporters say the bill is a tortuous piece of legislation, riddled with potential loopholes, but the intent is clear: mounted fox-hunting, fox-baiting and hare-coursing will be a criminal offence in Scotland punishable by a £5,000 fine or up to six months in jail. There will be no compensation for those affected by the ban.

As the anti-hunt lobby celebrated last night, rural campaigners said they could circumvent the legislation and would challenge it in the courts.

It was a day of angry protests and impassioned, sometimes farcical debate, with Basil Brush puppets brandished in the chamber and celebrity chef Clarissa Dickson Wright stalking the streets of Edinburgh to drum up support for the hunting lobby.

There are 10 mounted fox hunts in Scotland, half of them based in the border regions, and they employ around 3,000 people. Hunting does not have the same elitist image as it does in the south, but the Scottish public has been overwhelmingly supportive of a ban, and the bill has been seen as a further test of Holyrood's willingness to ignore Westminster and pursue its own course. Pressure was growing on Downing Street last night to bow to its devolved administration and follow suit.

'This is one of those defining moments in the history of UK parliaments,' said Graham Isdale of the Scottish campaign against hunting with dogs. 'It is a momentous occasion because Scotland is taking a lead in the UK, in the rest of Europe, and possibly in the rest of the world.'

Opponents say the bill is nothing more than destructive symbolism. 'This is an attack by urban politicians on the rural way of life and it will be challenged,' said Noel Collins of the Rural Rebels.

By early yesterday morning huntsmen were rousing their dogs for hunts across the country before descending on the border town of Kelso where a crowd of more than 1,000 gathered. 'No surrender. We will never be beaten!' shouted Sam Butler, chairman of the Campaign for Hunting, as the crowd – tweed-clad and spoiling for a fight – roared their approval and the dogs among them whined and yelped.

David Thomas, spokesman for the federation of Welsh packs, from Llandrindod, mid-Wales, warned there would be a revolution if Westminster tried to copy Scotland's lead.

'We are prepared to fight for our way of life and even die for it. You will not need to send envoys to Palestine or go to Africa to sort out problems there, Mr Blair, because there'll be too much trouble here,' he said. 'There'll be rivers of blood in the countryside just because I want to get on a horse and hunt a fox.'

The protests continued in Edinburgh, as MSPs gathered on the Mound for the start of the debate. The anti-hunt lobby stood vigil outside, draping police barriers with graphic images of dead foxes.

'This is such a huge occasion for us,' said Susan Small, 27, from

Edinburgh, an anti-hunt campaigner. 'We are taking a hugely symbolic step. Scotland is saying to the world that it does not accept an outdated and barbaric practice. Who knows where this could now lead?'

As the anti-hunt lobby celebrated last night, rural campaigners said they could circumvent the legislation and would challenge it in the courts

---

Inside the chamber, MSPs grimly ploughed their way through more than 100 amendments covering everything from exemptions for dog walkers whose pets inadvertently kill wild animals to compensation and gamekeepers.

The bill was first introduced in late 1999 by the Labour MSP Mike Watson. An independent study commissioned by the Scottish executive in 2000 concluded that up to 300 jobs would be lost in rural communities. In July last year the parliament's rural development committee decided not to endorse the general principles of the bill but two months later it passed the first stage in parliament.

Under the legislation, anyone who deliberately hunts a wild mammal with a dog is committing an offence. There are numerous exceptions, including preventing the spread of disease, and supporters of the bill say they may leave the door open for fox-hunting in some form.

Yesterday Simon Hart, the Countryside Alliance's director of campaign for hunting, said policing the ban would be practically impossible: 'It is a legislative nightmare and the police have better things to do than become involved in enforcing this.'

In England, MPs backed a ban on fox-hunting by 373 to 158 in December 2000, but the bill fell for lack of time in committee stage in the Lords. In May 2001, Labour's election manifesto promised a free vote on the issue and a commitment to introduce a bill was included in the Queen's speech in June last year.

The former sports minister Tony Banks said the government's credibility now rested on it introducing a ban in the rest of the UK. 'This is going to make a nonsense of the fact that we have an enormous majority in the House of Commons to ban hunting with dogs,' he said. 'Quite frankly the government has got to deliver. There is no excuse whatsoever. The credibility of the government is beginning to hang on this.'

A series of defiant hunts has been planned across Scotland today. 'This is going to be fought all the way,' said David Barnett, huntmaster with the Fife fox hounds. 'This is not the end of fox-hunting. This is not over.'

© Guardian Newspapers Limited 2002

Inherent cruelty of hunting with dogs

Information from the League Against Cruel Sports

Like all hunting with hounds, fox-hunting is designed to be cruel. Hounds are bred for stamina, providing the 'sport' of a lengthy chase. The fox is forced to run as far and as fast as it can until exhausted, when the hounds will catch and kill it. Hunters claim that the fox is killed instantly, but evidence has shown again and again that the fox is just as likely to be torn apart alive. Hunts can kill 20,000 foxes and their cubs annually.

In many parts of Britain the brown hare population is under great pressure due mainly to modern intensive farming. And yet, the species continues to be hunted and killed by packs of hounds and coursed by greyhounds simply for 'sport'. About 1,650 hares are killed annually by hunting by the registered packs and about 250 by the registered coursing clubs. Much larger numbers are killed by illegal coursing.

Although hunting deer with hounds has been illegal in Scotland for over 30 years, it still continues in England. Hunts chase and kill approximately 120 red deer every year. A stag hunt may last for over eight hours as the hunts select the strongest deer to provide the best chase.

Badgers are one of Britain's best-loved animals, and although fully protected by law from digging and baiting, they are still persecuted by a minority of criminals who kill as many as 10,000 animals every year. Mink hunting is a summer bloodsport. When mink are scented there is a chase by the hounds. If caught on the ground or in the water, the mink is torn apart by the hounds.

That dogs can be bred for speed to outmatch their quarry is proven by hare coursing. In this activity the greyhounds or lurchers used quickly overhaul the hare. The cruelty here is of a different form to that of the hound sports. Were fast dogs used in the hunting of fox or deer, the spectacle would end very quickly indeed with either the death or escape of the quarry. It is noticeable that where, for practical reasons, a quick kill is necessary (poaching) dogs bred for pace (e.g. lurchers) are used.

If fast-running dogs were used on a fox hunt the chase would be over within minutes. This would not provide the good cross-country gallop for which hunt subscribers pay. Each form of hunting has its own technique for extending the chase over and above that which would be natural in a predator versus prey situation. Thus it can be shown that the objective of hunting is not a quick chase and a swift kill, but the provision of entertainment. Therefore the suffering of the quarry can be shown to be 'unnecessary', i.e. the deliberate infliction of cruelty.

• The League Against Cruel Sports considers that the hunting of wild mammals with dogs is a cruel and unnecessary sport which has no place in modern Britain.

• The above information is from the League Against Cruel Sports' web site which can be found at www.league.uk.com Alternatively, see page 41 for their address details.

© 2000 League Against Cruel Sports Ltd.

Fox-hunting

Questions and answers. Information from Animal Aid

What are Animal Aid's views on this issue?

Animal Aid are opposed to all forms of animal cruelty – and we therefore strongly oppose hunting. Hunting with hounds has no place in modern Britain. It should have ended years ago along with cock-fighting, bear-baiting and dog-fighting.

When animal cruelty is portrayed by some as a 'sport' to get pleasure from it debases society and promotes even more animal cruelty. It is not just foxes and other wildlife who suffer. Horses and dogs are also victims of hunting – viewed simply as 'sporting accessories' many sustain fatal injuries during the gruelling chase.

What is its future?

You only need to look at the opinion polls:

- Almost two-thirds of the British electorate believe the Government should ban fox-hunting before the next general election. (NOP Solutions poll, PA 13/6/00)
- In a recent MORI poll, 65% supported a ban, with support being even higher among Labour supporters at 73%. (*The Economist*, June 2001)
- Two-thirds of MPs have already voted for a ban.
- 77 per cent of rural dwellers and 84 per cent of urban people disapprove of fox-hunting. (1997 Gallup poll for the *Daily Telegraph*)
- A MORI poll conducted on the Countryside March in 1998 revealed that only 40 per cent attended primarily because of the hunting issue.

The bloodsports fraternity are fighting a losing battle. They are grasping at straws with talk of inflated job losses, infringements of their rights and the countryside apparently falling into ruin. At the end of the day they have hundreds

of excuses for hunting but not one justification.

It is claimed that opposition to hunting is a left-wing, class issue?

People of all social classes oppose hunting. They oppose it not out of class envy but because they can see it is a cruel and perverted pastime. It is, however, true that fox-hunting has continued to this day purely as a result of the wealth and influential nature of the minority who partake in.

In an NOP poll commissioned by Channel 4, it was not just Labour voters in favour of an end to this bloodsport, 42% of Tory supporters also wanted an outright ban (PA 13/6/00).

Why do people go hunting?

Hunting is the exercise of power over a vulnerable prey. This is the source of pleasure it provides for those whose own lives and self-image are inadequate. There is also the element of social bonding.

A 10-year Oxford University study found that only half of the Hunt Masters questioned mentioned fox control as any justification for their 'sport'. 82% claimed that the hunt's main role was as 'a recreational and social force embodying a traditional rural pastime'.

How does the hunted fox suffer?

Every part of a fox-hunt is cruel – from the chase, to the dig-out, to the kill. There is no 'quick nip to the back of the neck' in hunting. Lead hounds will snap at any part of the running fox, before the pack rip it to pieces. If the fox manages to go to ground, then it will be forced to fight with terriers for hours before being hauled out and, if lucky, shot.

Copper the fox made national headlines. After being chased, and caught, by the Chiddingford, Leconfield and Cowdray Hunt hounds, he managed to bolt down a rabbit hole. Luckily, hunt saboteurs were close by and physically blocked the hounds from Copper, using a policeman's helmet.

Copper had suffered bite wounds to his rear flanks and was losing blood from his penis due to kidney damage caused during the stress and

exhaustion of the long run from the hounds. The vet was able to offer scientific evidence that hunted foxes undergo pathological stress, a level of suffering so intense that they can die even if they succeed in escaping the jaws of the hounds. He was quoted as saying: 'I have never seen such trauma in a dog, even a badly injured one.'

Post-mortems commissioned by the Home Office on four foxes killed by hunting revealed that there was evidence of multiple bite wounds to the face, head, rib cage, heart, lungs and stomach (*The Observer*, 11/6/00).

What are the humane alternatives – it is claimed that hunting with hounds is necessary to control fox numbers?

The whole point of hunting is that the 'chase' lasts as long as possible. This is why the hounds are bred for stamina, not speed. There have also been numerous cases where hunts have provided artificial earths to encourage foxes to breed to provide 'sport'. Recently the International Fund for Animal Welfare (IFAW) secretly filmed an employee of the Beaufort Hunt feeding fox cubs (*The Observer*, 11/6/00).

Furthermore, killing foxes has no lasting results. Foxes are territorial animals – if one fox is killed another soon moves into its place from a surrounding area. Foxes also control their own population.

The fox's diet of rabbits and rats actually makes it an asset to most farmers. A 1996 MAFF booklet stated that only 0.4% of lambs who die do so due to accidents, dog attacks, and all other animal predation – which includes being taken by foxes.

There are estimated to be 250,000 adult foxes in the UK, producing about 400,000 cubs a year, most of which will die in their first year of life. Humans kill about 400,000 foxes a year so a ban on fox-hunting, which kills about 20,000 a year at most, will have little impact.

The pro-hunt lobby claim that a ban would devastate the countryside and lead to job losses.

Countryside Alliance literature

claims that '15,900 people whose jobs directly depend on fox-hunting would be out of work.'

The Ministry of Agriculture recently declared this figure to be a gross exaggeration. There are about 330 hunts in the UK, each employing about 3 people – making a total of about 1,000 employees.

Hunters claim that once a fox has gone to ground 'it is usually left – except to be dug up and destroyed humanely' – is this true?

If a fox manages to find refuge in an unblocked earth, the hunt employ terrier men who will put their terriers down the earth to force the fox into the open to be re-hunted, or attack the fox underground while the men dig down through the soil to catch the terrified animal. Once they have dug the fox out, the terrier men are supposed to shoot it, but many will simply give it a blow with a spade. It is not unusual (although against fox-hunting 'rules') for the fox to be thrown alive to the waiting hounds.

Doesn't the image of hunt saboteurs perhaps negate their cause?

The dictionary gives a definition of sabotage as 'to render useless' and that is precisely what hunt saboteurs aim to do – to render the hunt useless

---

The public will not accept anything less than an outright ban which will see this bloodsport relegated to its rightful place – the history books

---

in their attempts to hunt down and kill wild animals.

Hunt saboteurs use non-violent direct action such as hunting horns and voice calls to try and gain control of the hounds. Scent maskers are also used to disguise the scent of the fox.

When it comes down to 'image' – seeing 30-plus people on horse-back, in all their regalia, intent on hunting down and killing a terrified animal – we know who has the image problem! Hunt saboteurs may not have PR gurus working overtime for them like the Countryside Alliance, but their aims are sincere and the majority of the public know this.

Whilst the present government quibbles about the ins and outs of a ban, thousands of foxes and other wild animals will be chased to a violent and bloody death. As long as this continues there will be hunt saboteurs prepared to put themselves in the front line to protect our wildlife.

Do Animal Aid believe that the government will ever ban hunting?

The government cannot withstand the will of the public. Hunting with hounds is one of the main issues on which the present government will be judged. The public will not accept anything less than an outright ban which will see this bloodsport relegated to its rightful place – the history books.

● The above information is from Animal Aid's web site which can be found at www.animalaid.org.uk Alternatively, see page 41 for their address details.

© Animal Aid

This is fox-hunting

Information from the Countryside Alliance

Fox-hunting is the pursuit of the wild fox with a pack of hounds. Man has been controlling foxes since he started to farm animals, but the hunting of foxes with hounds for sport became popular over two hundred years ago.

The fox is a pest and its population needs to be controlled. Individuals and organisations concerned with farming and the management of the countryside recognise this fact. Responsible fox management includes maintaining a healthy population at a level at which it can thrive without threatening livestock or other wildlife.

Fox-hunting is the most natural method of management: by its nature, it takes out the old, sick and injured foxes, and there is no risk of wounding. If the fox is caught, it is killed within seconds. If the fox goes to ground, it will either be left unharmed or the landowner may ask that it be killed by the hunt's terrierman. The strict rules governing terrier work laid down by the Masters of Foxhounds' Association (MFHA) ensure there is no unnecessary suffering.

Fox-hunting does not just help control fox numbers. Landowners with an interest in fox-hunting plant and maintain coverts, woodlands and copses for the benefit of all wildlife. Few farmers want to see the fox exterminated, but those who support hunting are more inclined to tolerate foxes on their land, as long as their numbers are controlled.

The fox

In rural areas of the UK, the red fox is in very good shape. After two hundred years of organised hunting, it is a well-conserved species. The British fox commands respect, but should not command sentimentality. Being an opportunist predator, the fox will kill poultry, wildfowl, newborn lambs and piglets beyond the needs of its staple diet of small wild mammals, insects and worms.

The fox is a hunter and covers considerable distances hunting for food or in search of a mate. Like all wild animals when threatened, the fox attempts to put an adequate 'flight distance' between itself and a potential enemy. This is a natural survival instinct.

Hunting the fox

Each hunt has its own designated area called the hunt country. The hunt meets at a predetermined place and moves off to a 'draw', a particular woodland or other habitat where foxes are likely to be found.

The only people involved with the hunting of the fox are the huntsman and his assistants, called Whippers-In. Mounted followers (the Field), under the control of the Field Master, are kept far enough away from the hounds to ensure they can work unhindered. Between 30 and 40 hounds (15 and 20 'couples') hunt on a given day.

Hounds are bred for intelligence, speed, stamina, voice and 'nose' (sense of smell). They follow the scent of a fox, which may be quite some distance away. When the fox is killed, the pack will often eat the corpse. This has led to the false belief that the hounds tear a live fox to pieces. This is a myth.

Seasons

Hunting is the only form of fox control that recognises a closed season.

Autumn hunting: August/ September – October

Foxes may be less than a year old but are, by this time, fully grown, and living and hunting independently. The objectives of autumn hunting are to cull some foxes and to disperse others, ensuring there are not too many in one area. Hounds hunt by instinct but during this period they learn to hunt only foxes.

Fox-hunting: November – March/ April

The duration of the season varies according to the nature of the farming in the area.

Call-outs: usually spring

A farmer who is losing lambs, piglets or poultry may ask the Hunt to track and kill the guilty fox. This is responsible work, not sport.

'There is no doubt . . . that foxes can be damaging and indiscriminate predators of birds and other animals . . . Control methods must remain available to those suffering economic damage from foxes.'

(Labour Party policy document *Wildlife in the Countryside*, 1991)

Questions and answers

Surely, a ban on hunting would benefit the fox?

'The trouble is that people see pictures of cowering foxes, feel sympathy for the fox, and then immediately conclude that fox-hunting should be banned. There's no real thought about what effect such a ban would in fact have on foxes. Of course, what would happen would be that far more would be shot, trapped and gassed.'

(Jim Barrington, former Executive Director of the League Against Cruel Sports)

Is the case for fox control overstated?

No. Fox predation causes significant lamb losses. Scientific estimates vary from 0.5% to 5.2%. Even at 2%, the cost to a typical hill farmer with 1,500 ewes is over £1,000. Without control, predation would increase considerably.

What would be the consequences of a ban on fox-hunting?

15,900 people whose jobs directly depend on fox-hunting would be out of work. Some 14,000 foxhounds would have no future as these working pack dogs would not make suitable pets. There would be less incentive for farmers to conserve wildlife habitat.

Is draghunting an alternative to fox-hunting?

No. The Masters of Draghounds' Association states: 'We strongly refute claims that draghunting is an alternative to foxhunting. Drag-hunting is an exciting equestrian sport in its own right, but is totally different to any other type of hound sport. It plays no role in the management of the red fox, which many farmers regard as a pest.'

Is fox-hunting a popular sport?

Yes. There are 194 registered packs of foxhounds in the UK followed by more than 50,000 riders and over 110,000 foot or car followers.

Come fox-hunting

If you would like to follow a hunt, contact the Countryside Alliance for assistance. Foot followers may be asked to pay a daily 'cap' of £1 or £2. Mounted followers pay between £25 and £70 per day. Some Hunts run 'Newcomers' Days' as an introduction to the sport for a minimal fee.

Foot followers should wear warm and waterproof clothing. Correct dress for mounted followers can vary and the Hunt Secretary should be consulted in advance of your first visit.

Code of conduct

Fox-hunting is controlled by the Masters of Fox Hounds' Association, which has strong sanctions to enforce its rules. Each hunt has Masters who are responsible for organising hunting, and ensuring that the MFHA Rules and the Code of Conduct are followed. Hunting depends on the goodwill of farmers who welcome the hunt, and followers must behave accordingly.

● The above information is from the Countryside Alliance's web site which can be found at www.countryside-alliance.org Alternatively, see page 41 for their address details.

© Countryside Alliance

Do foxes need controlling?

Information from the Hunt Saboteurs' Association

Quite simply, no. Artificial control of foxes by hunting, shooting, snaring etc. is neither necessary nor useful. Foxes, as with many wild animals, have their own biological method of population control. They will breed up to, but not over, the optimum level sustainable by their local environment.

Thus in areas where the fox population is high or food is scarce, vixens will breed small litters of cubs, whereas in areas where the opposite is the case, a larger litter will result.

Obviously then, when humans take a hand by killing foxes in an attempt at control, one of the main results will be that they will breed faster to compensate. This has been shown time and again in scientific studies, most notably in the study conducted by Dr Ray Hewson which found that when foxes were left unpersecuted the population level remained stable.

Far from being 'overrun with foxes' as hunters would have us believe, if foxes were not controlled in any way the only difference it would make is to produce a healthier fox population at the same level.

Even if fox control were necessary, it is difficult to imagine a less effective way of carrying it out than hunting. After a study by Dr Stephen Harris of Bristol University in 1997 it was reckoned that fox-hunts kill around 2.5% of Britain's foxes every year. As overseas studies on rabies control have shown that fox populations can withstand an annual mortality rate of 70%, the hunters have a very long way to go before they can claim to be an effective method of control.

(Extract from 'Foxhunting' by the HSA)

● The above information is from the Hunt Saboteurs' Association's web site which can be found at www.huntsabs.org.uk

© *Hunt Saboteurs' Association (HSA)*

Support for a ban

Despite the assertions of the Countryside Alliance, support for a ban on hunting is still running strong.

In a poll conducted by MORI for the *Economist* magazine in June 2001, they found that the public supported the ban by a margin of nearly two to one. (They polled 1,010 people interviewed throughout Great Britain in early June to report on a number of policies that have been considered by the Labour Government, and asked whether or not the people interviewed would support or oppose each one.)

Dodgy polls

The Countryside Alliance claim falling support based on polls with biased questioning and with three options (ban, licence or self-regulation) instead of two (ban or not).

For example, in April, they quoted approvingly an NOP poll with the biased wording: 'A bill now before Parliament could result in hunting being controlled by a new independent regulatory authority rather than it being made a criminal offence. The authority would be appointed by the Home Secretary and its members and Chairman approved by Parliament. Given the choice, which one of these options would you be most likely to support?

- All hunting to be controlled by a regulatory authority.
- All hunting to be made a criminal offence.
- All hunting to be remain as it is, subject to self-regulation.'

Professor Clive Nancarrow, Professor in Marketing Research at Bristol Business School, said, 'As an academic specialising in marketing research, I have some concerns about the wording of the poll question and the conclusions being drawn from it.

1) The phrasing of the introduction to the question may have swayed response. The introduction to the question relatively heavily features the option of hunt regulation by a regulatory authority and who would be involved. In my opinion, there is no need for this

introduction to the question if one wishes the question and options presented to be perceived as totally neutral. One could argue that to be seen to be fair all three response options need expanding or none at all.

2) The response option "All hunting to be made a criminal offence" I believe, breaks the trend in questioning over the years and so makes valid historical comparisons impossible. Previous polls have simply referred to a ban.

3) There may be some confusion given the three options presented to respondents repeatedly refer to "all hunting" rather than "hunting with dogs". Some respondents might think this includes certain types of shooting. This might invalidate the question to some extent.

The Countryside Alliance claim falling support based on polls with biased questioning and with three options (ban, licence or self-regulation) instead of two (ban or not)

'Because of the significant differences in wording of this poll to past ones, no real conclusion in my view can be drawn about public opinion trends on support for or opposition to a ban.'

Even Ivor Stocker, Chairman of NOP, said that NOP had not approved the Countryside Alliance comparison. He said that the different polls asked different questions and that no comparison was possible between them.

Increased desperation

On June 22, the Countryside Alliance issued a press release boasting that a Sky TV internet poll showed a 52%:48% lead against a hunting ban. But this was after they rigged the poll by emailing thousands of their supporters, in the UK and abroad, to urge them to log on to the internet site to vote.

In the absence of genuine evidence, they are forced to rely on polls where internet users opt in to have their say.

- The above information is an extract from the League Against Cruel Sports' web site which can be found at www.league.uk.com Alternatively, see page 41 for their address details.

© 2001 League Against Cruel Sports Ltd.

Polls show public opposition to hunt ban

Information from the Countryside Alliance

A new review by the Countryside Alliance reveals that public support for a hunting ban is at its lowest for ten years. Furthermore a leading animal charity has been criticised by the ASA for claiming that polls consistently show support for a ban. A recent MORI poll by the Campaign for Protection of Hunted Animals (CPHA) is shortly to be subject to a complaint to the Market Research Society for polling bias. The main poll findings of 2001 were:

1. NOP vets poll, July 2001

(1000 members of the Royal College of Veterinary Surgeons)

- 63% of rural vets oppose a ban on hunting on welfare grounds. Only 30% support a ban.
- On the subject of the Government's last Hunting Options Bill 66% of rural vets supported the continuation of hunting with dogs. (Either subject to statutory regulation (32%), or self-regulation subject to independent supervision (34%).) Only 24% of those questioned supported the 'total ban' option.
- 79% of rural vets consider that fox control is necessary in rural areas, only 15% saying that it isn't.

2. NOP national poll, April 2001

- 36% of those questioned wished all hunting to be controlled by a new regulatory authority, 22% still preferred all hunting to remain subject to its own existing system of self-regulation, but only 37% opted for it to be made a criminal offence.

3. NOP poll of rural Wales, October 2001

- Respondents were asked a range of questions on the future of hunting: Whether it should:
  a) made a criminal offence – this attracted 38% of the vote (but only 33% in areas described by respondents as rural).
  b) be allowed to continue under a system of government licensing: this attracted 25% of the vote.
  c) be allowed to continue under a system of self-regulation subject to independent supervision, 23% overall rising to 26% in areas describing themselves as rural.
  d) be allowed to continue without supervision attracted 11% of the vote overall rising to 13% in areas classing themselves as rural.
- In line with other polls recently taken this meant that 59% overall of those questioned stated that hunting with dogs should continue under some form of regulation, this figure rising to 65% in areas describing themselves as rural.

4. ASA adjudication against the RSPCA

- Several members of the public complained about an advertisement in the national press in February 2001 in which the RSPCA claimed that 'Independent polls have consistently shown that most people agree with us [that the majority of people want hunting banned]'.
  Referring to a number of recent polls, including an NOP poll for Channel 4 which showed less than 50% supported a ban, the ASA

These polls show that not only do the public not feel that a ban is needed or justified, but also that expert veterinary opinion considers it would be bad for animal welfare

---

agreed that the advertisement was inaccurate and asked the advertisers not to repeat the claim.

Commenting on these findings Simon Hart, Director of the Campaign for Hunting, said 'opponents of hunting have consistently claimed that their mandate for a ban is based on overwhelming public opposition to hunting. These polls show that not only do the public not feel that a ban is needed or justified, but also that expert veterinary opinion considers it would be bad for animal welfare.

'The results show that the public have seen through the deliberately misleading propaganda peddled by opponents of hunting to take the view that providing it is properly regulated and accountable, then hunting should be allowed to continue.'

Notes:

Poll 1 – commissioned by the Countryside Alliance for the *Daily Telegraph*. The poll was carried out by NOP Consumer between the dates 9th-19th July 2001. One thousand interviews took place amongst a random selection of vets (all members of the RCVS).

Poll 2 – commissioned by the Countryside Alliance. Conducted by NOP Consumer between 20th and 22nd April 2001. The poll asked 1000 adults which of the likely outcomes of the Government options Bill they would be most likely to support.

Poll 3 – commissioned by the Countryside Alliance (Wales). The poll, which was conducted by NOP between 10th and 21st October 2001, sought the opinions of 1000 residents of rural Wales on a range of issues.

Britain's illegal blood sport boom

Barbarism in the countryside

They meet every Sunday in gangs of up to 40, assembling at secret rural locations across Britain. Some of the men are armed with shotguns; some wear balaclavas. Many drive offroad vehicles and have travelled hundreds of miles for the illegal meet, which has been arranged over mobile phones. Their dogs, mostly lurchers, bark.

This is illegal hare coursing, a craze that is being dubbed 'the new dog fighting'. More than a dozen such events have taken place recently. The aim is simple: to bet on how many hares your dog can kill.

Once on a farm, the gang release their dogs, which race through crops or livestock searching for their prey, the brown hare. If a hare is spotted, it is normally only a few seconds before it is caught and killed. Some of the men cheer. If it is their dog that has killed the hare, they stand to make a lot of money.

Tomorrow, legal hare coursing and fox-hunting resume after a 10-month ban on blood sports since the outbreak of foot-and-mouth disease.

But illegal coursing is still big business. Up to £20,000 can change hands in one day. The best dogs can win their owners more than £40,000.

The fad presents problems for farmers, many of whom are still recovering from the effects of foot and mouth. The gangs trash crops, harm livestock and damage property. They also try to intimidate farmers who take action against them.

In the past few months, meetings have occurred in Sussex, Oxfordshire, Cambridgeshire, Lincolnshire, Essex, Humberside and East Anglia. In Kent, more than 25 farms have reported damage from coursing. One farmer in Kent said: 'I was threatened and warned that they knew which car my wife drove. Other farmers who have told police have found their barns alight. They drove across my fields, ruining my crops and scaring my livestock.'

Hare coursing even attracts criticism from some who used to be involved in it. John Byrne said: 'I used to go out with a couple of mates to do some illegal coursing – we called it poaching with dogs. But now it's got bigger and better organised. There's a lot of money involved betting on which dog can kill the most hares. Legal coursing has rules, but this is terrible – the hares have no chance.'

> 'These people are abusing, tormenting and killing hares for the fun of it and this depravity should have no place in the Britain of 2001.'

Robert Jackson, MP for Wantage in Oxfordshire, where there have been many problems with illegal hare coursing, has raised the issue in the Commons. He said: 'For landowners it is a problem and farmers have been threatened. Hare coursing with trespass has become a favourite weekend occupation of substantial numbers of rough urban dwellers, who will drive hundreds of miles for a day's "sport". The behaviour of such people towards farmers, the police and anybody who might get in their way is distinctly intimidatory.'

Douglas Batchelor, chief executive of the League Against Cruel Sports, said: 'All hare coursing is cruel and unnecessary, but the illegal meets are the most worrying. These people are abusing, tormenting and killing hares for the fun of it and this depravity should have no place in the Britain of 2001.'

• By Antony Barnett, Public Affairs Editor

• This article first appeared in *The Observer*, 16 December 2001.

Hunting must not be stuck in the past for ever

Fox-hunters need to adapt and give ground to be accepted, argues Rupert Isaacson

The recent resumption of fox-hunting has, predictably, seen the opening of a new anti-hunting season in Parliament. Of course, there are other rural issues to which these MPs could be giving their attention. Consider the report from the Policy Commission on Farming and Food of two weeks ago that is calling for sweeping changes to farming in the wake of foot and mouth.

This report argues that there is a pressing need for subsidising quality food, preferably of organic or at least natural production. Wedded to this would be subsidies for landowners towards conservation and environmental projects, the idea being that conservation and healthy food production should go hand in hand. This could revolutionise and re-energise both rural life and the lives of urban consumers.

Sadly, there is but one rural issue that excites New Labour MPs: the campaign to ban hunting.

As a fox-hunter, I don't want to see a ban. But I am faced with a dilemma. On the whole, I agree with those who argue that hunting is cruel. It involves chasing an animal to its death, albeit a quick one.

Could, or should, hunting change? It is a question that has to be answered, if only so that we could at last shelve the issue and allow Parliament to move on to other issues, such as the positive and practical suggestions of the Curry Report.

Do we really need to kill foxes? Most people, even the Government, agree that we do. Myself, I wonder. Ecologists say the British fox population could healthily absorb an annual cull of 75 per cent. The present combined annual cull – of hunting with hounds, shooting and road deaths – comes nowhere near that figure. Seen from this point of view, our efforts at fox control are just a drop in the ocean.

It's a tricky one, however. In upland areas – such as mid-Wales or the Lakes – the combined efforts of regular hunts, gun packs (where hounds drive foxes out of a wood towards a waiting line of guns), and keepers provide effective local fox control.

In Leicestershire, where I spent

> *Could, or should, hunting change? It is a question that has to be answered*

my hunting boyhood, foxes are not the same kind of pest. Sure, I remember waking up and finding the chicken house awash with feathers and blood, or another goose gone from the flock. But these losses were of no economic importance for us. Down our way, and over much of lowland Britain, foxes were (and still are) actively encouraged as a game species.

From a wildlife perspective, this is a good thing. As the ecologist and botanist Dr David Bellamy says: 'It is my firm belief that hunting, shooting and fishing play a vital role in the conservation and management of our wildlife and countryside.'

Although hunts look after far less woodland than, say, pheasant shoots, a Countryside Alliance-sponsored study found that more than 200,000 acres of woodland – more than 10 per cent of the woods within each of Britain's 185 fox-hunting counties – are maintained by hunts. By contrast, the government-run British Nature manages about 15,000 acres.

Then there are the hedgerows. Hunts do a lot of hedge-laying for free. According to the RSPB, well-laid hedgerows are 'often the most significant wildlife habitat over large stretches of lowland UK', and are

home to 'over 600 plant species, 1,500 insects, 65 species of bird and 20 different mammals'.

The new Policy Commission for Farming and Food's report suggests rewarding farmers 'who deliver attractive, healthy countryside and make the environment a selling point not a sore point for the industry'. In fact, Britain's hunting and shooting farmers have been doing this work voluntarily for years. The massacre of a pheasant shoot or the death of a hunted fox is sad, I know, but the link between conservation and hunting is clear.

But if I don't like killing things, why do I hunt? I love the ride, the hound work, the intimate connection with nature that hunting brings. But I prefer hunting in the USA, where, perhaps because of the lack of sheep farms and the more 'varminty' nature of the American countryside, landowners do not expect hunts to act as pest control units. So there is no terrier-work, no digging, no earth-stopping. If hounds lose the fox, the hunt tends to look for another one, rather than pursue the original quarry to its death.

American hunts conserve habitat just as their British counterparts do. But the kill rate is about four in 100, usually of mangy, sick or wounded (usually shot) animals, and this sits more easily with me.

Away from hill areas, I would like to see us hunt as the Americans do, without the intent to kill, and with no digging. Those who believe that hunts should provide fox control would dismiss this view, as would hard-line antis, for whom even chasing an animal is wrong. But I suggest it as a starting point for some dialogue about change.

The public perception of fox-hunters is of a minority with entrenched, traditional views. In fact, there is more open-mindedness than one might think.

As Michael Sagar, editor of *Hounds* magazine, puts it: 'So far, all our financial and human resources have had to go into defending hunting, and this makes us appear very reactionary. In an ideal world, the currently hostile government would give us five years, in which to find out what changes would make hunting acceptable to the wider

public and then to implement them.'

To be fair, the hunting establishment has made some small changes in recent years, such as banning 'holding up' (or keeping young foxes inside a wood where it is easier to kill them). But I still wonder if we are doing everything we can as fox-hunters to limit the suffering of the quarry on whom our strange ritual depends. And I worry that, if we refuse to give any real ground, then a ban might well be the eventual result, with disastrous consequences for conservation, and the endless blocking of other countryside issues.

Tom Beck, an American hunter and ecologist, summed it up neatly when he said that we need to 'bring a stronger social consciousness to our ideas as wildlife managers and hunters. We must change, or we will cease to exist.'

• Rupert Isaacson's *The Wild Host: The History and Meaning of the Hunt* (Cassell, £25), is available for £22 plus 1.99p, through Telegraph Books Direct, 0870 155 7222.

© *Telegraph Group Limited, London 2002*

Anti-hunt lobby gangs up on Blair

Animal welfare campaigners invoke Labour pledge on banning fox-hunting in campaign to reintroduce bill before time runs out

Tony Blair is being given just weeks to reintroduce a bill banning fox-hunting or face a campaign from the animal welfare lobby accusing him of betraying the people's trust.

The increasingly impatient lobby awaits a decision from the prime minister and advisers, including Lady Morgan, on how the Labour manifesto pledge, for a free vote on hunting early in the parliament, will be honoured.

Mr Blair is reluctant to risk the wrath of rural communities while they are starting to recover from the foot-and-mouth debacle. At prime minister's questions yesterday he again sidestepped pressure from

By Patrick Wintour, Chief Political Correspondent

Labour backbenchers to commit himself to reintroducing the bill.

'Anyone in this government who thinks they can brush this issue aside is making a very major misjudgment. It is about the good faith of the government'

Tony Banks, the leading anti-fox-hunting MP, said later: 'Anyone in this government who thinks they can brush this issue aside is making a very major misjudgment. It is about the good faith of the government. It's also about time some of the big players in the Labour party stopped thinking you should appease your enemies but piss off your friends big time.'

The political dilemma is moving up the agenda as the government must either reintroduce the fox-hunting bill which fell before the last election, or see the measure fall again for lack of time. With 25 weeks until the end of the session, backers of a ban stress that a decision to introduce a bill in the Commons must be made shortly.

So far, Mr Blair has stonewalled in public on his plans, but faces the embarrassment of seeing the Scottish first minister, John McConnell, rush a ban through the Scottish parliament in the next few weeks.

Ministers at Westminster are casting around for a solution, admitting privately that Mr Blair is reluctant to use the Parliament Act to overcome Lords opposition. There are also doubts over whether the Speaker is constitutionally entitled to invoke the act.

However, the RSPCA, a leading member of the Countdown To A Ban campaign, has secured an opinion from Nicholas Serle QC on legal procedure. The Parliament Act allows bills to become law if they have been passed by the Commons in two successive sessions though rejected in the same two sessions by peers. The only condition is that the bill going to the Lords must be exactly the same each time.

With most MPs backing a ban, the Commons is certain to return the bill to the Lords in the same form as last year. Last year peers rejected a ban at second reading, but the bill fell because of the election.

Ministerial sources say Mr Blair is reluctant to use the act believing the measure should be used sparingly. And he does not want a confrontation with the Lords.

The hunting ban campaign claims: 'With the position of the Lords appearing intractable it is unthinkable that the bill could become law in one session and without the use of the Parliament Act. This is the best opportunity the goverment has ... to see the ban on hunting with dogs introduced.'

The campaign claims the bill could be passed in the Commons during one day, and need not take more than five days in the Lords. If the bill were rejected by the Lords at second reading or amended in committee, the Parliament Act would be invoked immediately, the pro-ban MPs claim.

The act would be invoked automatically by the Speaker, and not by government, so relieving the pressure on Mr Blair to take the initiative.

All five ministers at the Department for Environment, Food and Rural Affairs, which is responsible for fox-hunting, support a ban. But lobbyists recognise that the highly political decision will be taken by Mr Blair and his advisers.

Apart from using the Parliament Act, Defra ministers have also floated a range of options to meet the manifesto commitment, but none of them with great enthusiasm. Alun Michael, the rural affairs minister responsible for fox-hunting, has looked at the possibility of 'an indicative vote in both houses', as a means of testing opinion. However, such a vote is likely merely to reconfirm that MPs overwhelmingly back a ban, while peers remain opposed.

More than 300 MPs have put their names to an early day motion on a ban. Advocates of the tactic claim peers might relent and back the compromise of fox-hunting under licence. Ministers have looked at fox-hunting being within a wider animal cruelty act. That move would defer the issue for two years, and is seen as a blatant delaying tactic.

Above all, Defra ministers argue that leaving the issue hanging around the domestic agenda for two more years would be the worst of all worlds.

Ministers have also sounded out Labour peers.

© *Guardian Newspapers Limited 2002*

Parliament and hunting

November 1997
Second reading. MPs voted 411 to 151 in favour of Mike Foster's bill outlawing pursuit of foxes, stags, hares and mink

March 1998
Countryside Alliance goes to London. Bill falls due to filibustering

July 1999
Blair revives the issue on BBC *Question Time*

June 2000
Lord Burns report concludes fox-hunting 'seriously compromises the welfare of the fox'. Jack Straw offers a three-alternatives bill which includes the status quo, a ban, or licensed hunting

December 2000
MPs back outright ban by 373 to 158, but Lords support status quo. Bill falls for lack of time in committee stage in the Lords

May 2001
Labour's election manifesto promises a free vote saying parliament will be allowed to reach a conclusion

June 2001
A commitment to introduce the bill included in the Queen's speech.

ADDITIONAL RESOURCES

You might like to contact the following organisations for further information. Due to the increasing cost of postage, many organisations cannot respond to enquiries unless they receive a stamped, addressed envelope.

Animal Aid
The Old Chapel
Bradford Street
Tonbridge, TN9 1AW
Tel: 01732 364546
Fax: 01732 366533
E-mail: info@animalaid.org.uk
Web site: www.animalaid.org.uk
Animal Aid is the UK's largest animal rights group and one of the longest established in the world. To receive information please send a large sae to the address above.

The Association of the British Pharmaceutical Industry (ABPI)
12 Whitehall
London, SW1A 2DY
Tel: 020 7930 3477
Fax: 020 7747 1414
Web site: www.abpi.org.uk
ABPI is the trade association for about a hundred companies in the UK producing prescription medicines.

British Humanist Association (BHA)
47 Theobald's Road
London, WC1X 8SP
Tel: 020 7430 0908
Fax: 020 7430 1271
E-mail: info@humanism.org.uk
Web site: www.humanism.org.uk
The BHA is the UK's leading organisation for people concerned with ethics and society, free from religious and supernatural dogma.

The British Union for the Abolition of Vivisection (BUAV)
16a Crane Grove
London, N7 8NN
Tel: 020 7700 4888
Fax: 020 7700 0252
E-mail: info@buav.org
Web site: www.buav.org
The BUAV opposes animal experiments. They believe animals are entitled to respect and compassion which animal experiments deny them. The BUAV campaigns peacefully for effective, lasting change by challenging attitudes and action towards animals worldwide.

Countryside Alliance
The Old Town Hall
367 Kennington Road
London, SE11 4PT
Tel: 020 7840 9200
Fax: 020 7793 8484
E-mail: info@countryside-alliance.org
Web site: www.countryside-alliance.org
The Countryside Alliance campaigns for rural livelihood.

Dr Hadwen Trust
84a Tilehouse Street
Hitchin, SG5 2DY
Tel: 01462 436819
Fax: 01462 436844
E-mail: info@drhadwentrust.org.uk
Web site: www.drhadwentrust.org.uk
The Dr Hadwen Trust is funding non-animal research into major health problems such as cancer, heart disease, meningitis and Alzheimer's disease.

FRAME (Fund for the Replacement of Animals in Medical Experiments)
Russell & Burch House
96-98 North Sherwood Street
Nottingham, NG14EE
Tel: 0115 958 4740
Fax: 0115 950 3570
E-mail: frame@frame.org.uk
Web site: www.frame.org.uk
FRAME considers that the current scale of live animal experimentation is unacceptable and should not be allowed to continue.

Hunt Saboteurs' Association (NWHSA)
PO Box 5254
Northampton, NN1 3ZA
Tel: 0845 450 0727
E-mail: info@huntsabs.org.uk
Web site: www.huntsabs.org.uk
Strongly opposed to all blood sports. They will try to answer requests for information if it doesn't appear elsewhere on their web site, but please check the rest of the site before requesting information.

Huntingdon Life Sciences
Woolley Road, Alconbury
Huntingdon, PE28 4HS
Tel: 01480 892000
Fax: 01480 590693
Web site: www.huntingdon.com
Huntingdon Life Sciences is one of the world's foremost product development companies.

League Against Cruel Sports
Sparling House, 83/87 Union Street
London, SE1 1SG
Tel: 020 7403 6155
Fax: 020 7403 4532
Web site: www.league.uk.com
Maintains a unique approach to the protection of wildlife – combining campaigning with conservation.

Research Defence Society (RDS)
58 Great Marlborough Street
London, W1F 7JY
Tel: 020 7287 2818
Fax: 020 7287 2627
E-mail: admin@rds-online.org.uk
Web site: www.rds-online.org.uk
RDS represents medical researchers in the public debate about the use of animals in medical research and testing.

Uncaged Campaigns
2nd Floor, St Matthew's House
45 Carver Street, Sheffield, S1 4FT
Tel: 0114 272 2220
Fax: 0114 272 2225
E-mail: uncaged.anti-viv@dial.pipex.com
Web site: www.uncaged.co.uk
Uncaged Campaigns represents the cutting edge of the movement against animal experiments.

Young People's Trust for the Environment
8 Leapale Road
Guildford, GU1 4JX
Tel: 01483 539600
Fax: 01483 301992
E-mail: info@yptenc.org.uk
Web site: www.yptenc.org.uk
Works to educate young people in matters relating to the conservation of the world's wild places and natural resources.

INDEX

ACKNOWLEDGEMENTS

The publisher is grateful for permission to reproduce the following material.

While every care has been taken to trace and acknowledge copyright, the publisher tenders its apology for any accidental infringement or where copyright has proved untraceable. The publisher would be pleased to come to a suitable arrangement in any such case with the rightful owner.

Overview
Animal welfare, © British Humanist Association (BHA), *Why animal rights?*, © Animal Aid, *Animal welfare and animal rights*, © Countryside Alliance, *Animal cruelty culture*, © The Daily Mail, June 2001.

Chapter One: Animal Experiments
Different views, © ABPI – The Association of the British Pharmaceutical Industry, *Introduction to animal experiments*, © The British Union for the Abolition of Vivisection (BUAV), *Some of the species used*, © The British Union for the Abolition of Vivisection (BUAV), *Popular misunderstandings*, © Huntingdon Life Sciences, *The use of animals by society*, © Biomedical Research Education Trust, *The debate about animal experiments*, © Uncaged Campaigns, *The hope, the challenge, the people*, © Research Defence Society (RDS), *Animal testing is a disaster*, © Guardian Newspapers Limited 2001, *Animals in medicines research*, © ABPI – The Association of the British Pharmaceutical Industry, *The benefits of animals in scientific research*, © Huntingdon Life Sciences, *Vivisection*, © Young People's Trust for the Environment (YPTENC), *Frequently asked questions*, © FRAME (Fund for the Replacement of Animals in Medical Experiments), *The use of animals in scientific procedures*, © Crown

Copyright is reproduced with the permission of the Controller of Her Majesty's Stationery Office, *Types of animals used in medical research*, © Research Defence Society (RDS), *The use of animals by you*, © Biomedical Research Education Trust, *Alternatives*, © Dr Hadwen Trust.

Chapter Two: Focus on Fox-hunting
Hunting – focus on the figures, © Countryside Alliance, *The Countryside Alliance's policy on welfare*, © Countryside Alliance, *Hunting with dogs*, © Crown Copyright is reproduced with the permission of the Controller of Her Majesty's Stationery Office, *Scotland bans fox-hunting*, © Guardian Newspapers Limited 2002, *Inherent cruelty of hunting with dogs*, © 2000 League Against Cruel Sports Ltd., *Fox-hunting*, © Animal Aid, *This is fox-hunting*, © Countryside Alliance, *Do foxes need controlling?*, © Hunt Saboteurs Association (HSA), *Support for a ban*, © 2001 League Against Cruel Sports Ltd., *Polls show public opposition to hunt ban*, © Countryside Alliance, *Britain's illegal blood sport boom*, © Guardian Newspapers Limited 2001, *Hunting must not be stuck in the past for ever*, © Telegraph Group Limited, London 2002, *Anti-hunt lobby gangs up on Blair*, © Guardian Newspapers Limited 2002.

Photographs and illustrations:
Pages 1, 24, 32, 37: Pumpkin House; pages 5, 14, 27, 30, 35, 38, 40: Simon Kneebone; pages 6, 29, 31, 33: Bev Aisbett; pages 9, 13, 19: Fiona Katauskas.

Craig Donnellan
Cambridge
April, 2002